The (even) Greater, Great Lakes Trivia Test

The Who, What, Where, When, Why and How of Michigan

Michael J. Thorp

SouThorp Publishers
Flint, Michigan

Michigan's State Motto

Si quaeris peninsulam amoenam cirumspice
"If you seek a pleasant peninsula, look about you"

Michael J Thorp's paraphrase
Si quaeris peninsulam amoenam habemus copiam eligendi.
"If you seek a pleasant peninsula, we have plenty to choose from"

SouThorp Publishers
Flint, Michigan

Published by

SouThorp Publishers

Flint, Michigan

Publisher's Cataloging-in-Publication-Data

Thorp, Michael J.

The (even) Greater Great Lakes Trivia Test II-The Who, What, Where, When, Why and How of Michigan/ Michael J. Thorp- Flint, Michigan: SouThorp Publishers, 2017.; cm.

ISBN-13: 978-1986379984
ISBN-10: 1986379981

I. Michigan-History-Miscellanea. 2. Great Lakes (North America) –Miscellanea. I. Title

FIRST EDITION

Layout & Design Steven D. Kimbrell

Printed in the United States of America

Dedication

For those who love a good, true story, for those who believe that what really happened is often stranger than what is made up, and especially for those who believe history is more than dates.

Also for Ginny, who makes everything go, and my other girls, Libby and Ella, their guys, TJ and Brett; and my grands, Emersyn and Evelyn; I can't imagine life without them.

Also by Michael J. Thorp

The Great, Great Lakes Trivia Test-
The Who, What, Where, When, Why and How of Michigan

The Legend of the Abominable Huckleberry
(or)
The Practically True Story of How the Huckleberry Railroad Got
its Name
(Children's book)

Michigan's Thumb Drive-
A Ride Around Michigan's Blue Water Highway

American Civil War Years: The Michigan Experience
(The Reenactor's Telling)
(Contributor)

Forward

The story of "The (Even) Greater, Great Lakes Trivia Test II: The Who, What, Why, Where, When and How of Michigan" starts on the radio! While this is my fourth book, I have spent decades as a broadcaster. Beginning with my first professional radio job in 1973 I have been on the air at radio and television stations all over the state of Michigan, as well as having hosted television and radio programs with a worldwide reach.

I have been a disc jockey, radio newsman, play by play announcer, voice over talent, television news anchor, reporter, producer, I have appeared in movies, advertising campaigns and billboards; I have done about all you can do at a radio or television station.

I am constantly looking for interesting stuff to talk about on air.

I hold a degree, from the University of Michigan-Flint in History, and have done post graduate in Historic Preservation. Basically, while my profession is broadcasting, my avocation is historian. I am fascinated by things that really happened. As I always say, you really can't make up stranger stories than things that really happened. And I have found so many stories about Michigan that are surprising that I want to tell.

As you can tell by my books I am a storyteller, I love to tell stories about things that really happened, especially about things that happened in Michigan; but where do the stories come from? I collect stories from many sources. Have you ever been in a restaurant and noticed the placemat has stories about the local community? I grab them and take them home to store them in a cardboard box. If you go to any tourist trap, visitors bureau, or road side park in the state you will find brochures about local sites and attractions; I save them in my box too. I cut stories out of the newspaper, magazines, and local historical society newsletters; and put them in my box. I collect, and read, local history books, old letters, diaries and more; just to get stuff to talk about on the air.

The, who, what, where, when, why and how in my title are the outline for a reporter, if you answer those six questions, you've got a story. These are the main questions of inquiry for any reporter, and the ones I use as the chapters of my trivia books.

So how did the first book start? Well, my cardboard box began to overflow. After all those years, since I was in high school, I had collected those tid-bits of history and tossed them into my box, and when we moved several years ago my wife, Ginny, asked me what I was going to do what that box. I had planned to move it, but it didn't sound like that was a good idea, so I wrote the "The Great, Great Lakes Trivia Test", just so I could get rid of the box. It was a great way to consolidate!

But there was a problem, I had too much in the box, and couldn't use all the good stories in book one. Plus, I just couldn't stop that old habit of grabbing brochures and placemats, cutting up newspapers and magazines and bringing them home. I'm just addicted I guess; it's impossible for me to just say no to history.

So in order to empty that old box, again, and please Ginny, here comes, "The (Even) Greater, Great Lakes Trivia Test II." This one is also chock full of great stories about the Great Lakes, its people and places, events and surprises. It has more stories, is a bit more in depth, but still only a page or less each for each. It is a Michigan history lesson like you have never seen, unless, of course, you read the first Great, Great Lakes Trivia Test.

I do still have a problem; I still haven't been able to empty that old box, and I keep adding to it. Sooner or later Ginny will once again say, "What are you going to do with that box"? Perhaps one day I will, have to write, "The Greatest Great Lakes Trivia Test; just to empty the box of course.

Take my test; by yourself or with friends and family, have fun, learn some fun stuff and enjoy!

Michael J. Thorp

Author
Broadcaster
Historian

Contents

Introduction

Ever since I published my first book, "The Great, Great Lakes Trivia Test", I wanted to add more stories to it. I just keep finding more interesting, enlightening and fascinating true stories about our Winter Water Wonderland, its people and history.

The story of Michigan is the story of lumberjacks, miners, trappers, race car drivers, auto pioneers, French explorers, Spanish raiders, sailing ships, wineries, cowboy heroes, digital age pioneers, early women pioneers, Revolutionary War generals, astronauts and the leader at the Little Big Horn. In short, Michigan history is American history.

I love telling these stories; they're what make Michigan unique. Many could only happen here in the Great Lakes State, with our diverse land and people. We think of Michigan as a manufacturing state, we build cars and trucks; even the Motor City and Vehicle City are in Michigan. But we also have mountains, inland seas, orchards, wine country, sailors and a robust fishing industry, mining, farms, cattle.

We have shipwrecks and islands, lighthouses and Native American long houses. Michigan boasts one of the longest bridges on earth and an old fashioned, coal fired, ferry that can take you and your car across Lake Michigan. The Great Lakes State contains places that look like Germany, Finland, and Greece; and three hundred year old cities.

Michigan was the site of Revolutionary War battles, one of the most famous battles of The War of 1812, we held Confederate prisoners in Michigan during the Civil War and German Prisoners during WWII.

The amazing wonder is that no matter where I look I see another interesting Michigan story I want to tell.

In my first book, I gave short answers to my trivia questions. Sometimes I had a potential answer that was one of the wrong choices that I could have and should have told the reader a bit more about. Many of the wrong answer were as interesting as the correct answers.

Maybe I was a little too succinct.

This time, "The (even) Greater, Great Lakes Trivia Test II" will differ a bit from the first one in that I will have more in depth and complete answers, to both the correct answer to my question, and even more information on the answers that are wrong; there are remarkable stories in both of them.

It gives me a chance to add a few more stories.

An example is the story of Michigan's first governor, Stevens T. Mason, often referred to as "the boy governor." He died quite young and was buried more than once; actually he was buried several times. In the first book I would likely have just given the answer; this time I will tell the story of each burial.

In a question about Michigan's connection with several Revolutionary War generals: Who was the first Governor of the Michigan Territory? I have stories about all three choices; Anthony "Mad Anthony" Wayne, Henry Dearborn and Arthur St. Clair. Plus I'll tell you why they called him "Mad" and if the moniker was deserved.

My goal is to get you interested enough in these stories, to ask yourself, "Did that really happen? Then go and look up more answers for yourself. That is what a historian is supposed to do, get people to ask their own questions, and encourage curiosity.

I want you to be inspired to "look it up."

That is a lesson from my Dad, L. P. "Jim" Thorp. When I was about 10 years old, he and I were watching a John Wayne movie called, "Back to Bataan." In that movie, the big voice announcer says that 80,000 U.S. troops surrendered to the Japanese, the largest capitulation of U.S. forces ever. I asked my Dad if that was true, and he gave me a great answer; he said, "Look it up lad, look it up."

I hope you have fun taking "The (even) Greater, Great Lakes Trivia Test II", testing how your knowledge of Michigan compares to your friends and family. I want you to learn about Michigan's fascinating history and its potential future. Always challenge yourself to ask questions, question my answers and, as my Dad said, when in doubt, "look it up, lad, look it up."

"Who?"

THE *(even)* GREATER, GREAT LAKES *(Who)* TRIVIA QUIZ

Who famously was supposed to have said, "Thank God for Michigan"?

    A. Henry Ford
    B. Kay Lani Rafko (Miss Michigan/Miss America)
    C. Abraham Lincoln

THE ANSWER IS C.
Our 16th President was reported to say, "Thank God for Michigan", when he saw the first Michigan troops marching down Pennsylvania Avenue. Michigan was the first western state to send troop after Lincoln had called for volunteers.

Henry Ford was born in Dearborn, MI and was the founder of Ford Motor Company.

Kay Lani Rae Rafko Wilson was Miss Michigan in 1987 and named Miss America in 1988. She is a Registered Nurse from Monroe, Michigan.

Who among these famous people is a Michigan native?

    A. George Armstrong Custer
    B. Christie Brinkley
    C. Aretha Franklin

THE ANSWER IS B.
Supermodel and businesswoman Christie Brinkley was born in Monroe Michigan. Col. Custer, though he too lived and married in Monroe, Mi. was born in New Rumley, Ohio. The Queen of Soul, Aretha Franklin, was born in Memphis, Tennessee but has lived in Detroit for many years.

There are some sayings in sports, especially in baseball, that have special meaning. For example when someone isn't hitting well they are said to be below the "Mendoza Line", or less than .200 batting average, (Named for Mario Mendoza, who played great defense for the Pittsburgh Pirates, Seattle Mariners, and Texas Rangers from 1975-79 but couldn't hit). Another famous saying is, "he was Wally Pipped."

Who was Wally Pipp and where did the, "he was Wally Pipped" saying come from?

A. He sang and danced the Pipp in his Cousin Gladys's back-up group the Pips.

B. Wally was a baseball star with the Yankees who was replaced in the line-up

C. He was an investor who lost millions in a scheme to find the lost continent of Atlantis

THE ANSWER IS B.

Wally Pipp grew up in Grand Rapids, MI where, like his father, he was a very good ball player. He played with the Detroit Tigers and Ty Cobb in 1913 and later was traded to the New York Highlanders, who became the Yankees while he was there. He won home run championships in 1916 and 1918. He was also a great fielder at first base.

In 1925, Pipp took a ball to the head and suffered headaches. On June 12, 1925 he had a headache and manager Miller Huggins gave him the day off to recover. He replaced him with a young man named Lou Gehrig who played for the next 2,130 games, or until 1939.

Wally Pipp went on to play in Cincinnati and finally retire in 1928. He moved back to Michigan where he hosted a radio show before Detroit Tiger games and made a living on the stock market. He even wrote a book about it, "Buying Cheap and Selling Dear."

Lou Gehrig was Wally Pipped himself by Ellsworth "Babe" Dahlgren who replaced him that day at Briggs Stadium in Detroit. The Briggs Stadium announcer told the fans that day, "Ladies and gentlemen, this is the first time Lou Gehrig's name will not appear on the Yankee lineup in 2,130 consecutive games." Tigers' fans gave Gehrig a standing ovation while he sat on the bench with tears in his eyes.

A graduate of Gaylord High, School the University of Michigan and MIT; he could juggle four balls while riding a unicycle. He was a brilliant mathematician and engineer and some call him the father of the digital age.

Who was the Michiganian who is known as the father of the digital age?

A. Charles Frederick Towar

B. Claude Shannon

C. Thomas Edison

4

THE ANSWER IS B.

Dr. Claude Shannon was born in 1916 in Petoskey in northern Michigan, but grew up in the little town of Gaylord. He loved erector sets as a boy and loved to tinker. As a boy, he strung a telegraph line from his house to a friends'.

In 1932, he graduated from Gaylord High and went on to the University of Michigan. While at the U of M he took an algebra class that looked at the work of a 19th century mathematician named George Boole. In Boole's work he used a 1, to designate a true statement and a 0 to designate a false statement.

Shannon remembered that familiar "1" and "0" in his later work and used it in his "Mathematical Theory of Communications" as a building block of today's digital technology.

Of course **Thomas Edison** was an extraordinary inventor who began his career publishing a paper on a train from his home in Port Huron.

Charles Frederick Towar worked with a lot of numbers, but was not the father of the digital age. He is the father of a childhood, school and old Scouting friend of the author. He graduated of the University of Michigan as a civil engineer and came to Flint in 1959 to work for the Flint schools. He was integral in the construction of schools and many College and Cultural Center buildings including; The Whiting Auditorium, the Sarvis Center and Sloan Museum.

As a side note, Mr. Towar was the Scoutmaster of Boy Scout Troop 43, at Flint's Civic Park School in 1972 when a fire all but destroyed the building. He and his Scouts went into the building and saved part of the school, including the Gym and Library, from flooding.

There is a house at 1805 Gratiot Avenue in Saginaw that was built in around 1911. It is now a museum dedicated to Theodore Roethke.

Who was Theodore Roethke and why is the house he grew up in a museum?

A. He was a distinguished poet and Pulitzer Prize winner.

B. He was a lumberman in Saginaw who donated land for parks and schools

C. Roethke was the inventor of sandpaper

THE ANSWER IS A.

Theodore Roethke was a poet who won the Pulitzer Prize for his poem, "The Waking" in 1954. He was born in Saginaw in 1908, and grew up in the house on Gratiot, now called the Theodore Roethke Home Museum. He graduated

Who

from Arthur Hill High School in Saginaw and the University of Michigan. He later taught at Michigan State College (now Michigan State University) and at colleges in Pennsylvania and Vermont before joining the faculty of the University of Washington at Seattle in 1947. Roethke died in Washington State in 1963 and is buried in Saginaw's Oakwood Cemetery.

HERE IS HIS PULITZER PRIZE WINNING POEM.

The Waking

I wake to sleep, and take my waking slow.
I feel my fate in what I cannot fear.
I learn by going where I have to go.

We think by feeling. What is there to know?
I hear my being dance from ear to ear.
I wake to sleep, and take my waking slow.

Of those so close beside me, which are you?
God bless the Ground! I shall walk softly there,
And learn by going where I have to go.

Light takes the Tree; but who can tell us how?
The lowly worm climbs up a winding stair;
I wake to sleep, and take my waking slow.

Great Nature has another thing to do
To you and me; so take the lively air,
And, lovely, learn by going where to go.

This shaking keeps me steady. I should know.
What falls away is always, and is near.
I wake to sleep, and take my waking slow.
I learn by going where I have to go.

This army general considered Michigan home, even though he was born in Ohio in 1832. He graduated from West Point in 1856 and was immediately sent to Detroit where his job was to oversee a lake survey. During the Civil War he served on General George McClelland's staff, was leader of the Second Michigan Infantry, and promoted to General as Gen. William Tecumseh Sherman's engineering officer: building hundreds of bridges during Sherman's famous march to the sea.

After the war he came back to Michigan to design and build seven lighthouses around the Great lakes and oversee over 100 more.

Who was this famous Michigan General?

A.   Mathew Schlinker
B.   Orlando Poe
C.   Thomas E. Selfridge

THE ANSWER IS B.

General Orlando Poe was an extraordinary engineer, trained at West Point. He oversaw the burning of Atlanta in the Civil War. He came home and built and designed many lighthouses including; Gross Point Lighthouse, Outer Island, Au Sable, Little Sable Point, South Manitou and New Presque Isle. All of General Poe's lighthouses are still lit and in use on the Great Lakes.

Thomas Selfridge was 1st Lieutenant Thomas E. Selfridge. Born in 1882 in San Francisco, California he graduated from United States Military Academy in 1903, 31st in a class of 96; Douglas MacArthur was first. Selfridge Air Force Base, located near Mount Clemens is named for him. He was killed in September 1908 while flying as a passenger with Orville Wright at Fort Myer, Virginia.

Matt Schlinker is a friend of the author. He is an auditor for General Motors and a long time Flint area activist. He has served on many boards and commissions including; the Flint Public Library Board and as a member of Flint City Council. He is married to Sherry and has a son and two grandchildren.

Who threw the first no hitter in Detroit Tigers' baseball history?

A.   George Mullin
B.   Jim Bunning
C.   Mickey Lolich

THE ANSWER IS A,

George Mullin, a right-handed pitcher who played fourteen seasons with the Detroit Tigers, from 1902–13 tossed the first Tigers no hitter. He also had five 20-win seasons, had a career record of 228-196 including a league, leading 29 wins in 1909. He helped the Tigers to three straight American League pennants, 1907–1909 and twice hit over .310 as a batter. Now that's a pitcher.

Who

"Jim" Bunning, who passed in 2017, was also Tigers pitcher of note. He played from1955 to 1971 compiling a 224-184 record. Bunning pitched a perfect game in 1964, and was inducted into the Baseball Hall of Fame in 1996. Bunning then went into politics and served in the U.S. House of Representatives and the U.S. Senate from 1987 to 2011.

Mickey Lolich was a left handed pitcher for the Tigers from 1963-1975. He actually was born a righty but a tricycle accident in early childhood forced him to throw left-handed. He always batted and writes right handed. His major league record was 217 -191.

He became a true Tiger hero in 1968 when he beat the St. Louis Cardinals in game 7 in the 1968 World Series. He was the 12th pitcher in history to win three games in a World Series and the last with three complete games in a series. Lolich helped the Tigers win game 2 by allowing only one run and by hitting the first and only home run of his 16-year career and game 7 by starting on only 2 days' rest.

After retirement he opened a doughnut shop in the Detroit area.

Who

In 1871, Michigan became the first state to make "Decoration Day" a holiday. It was an idea that came from the G.A.R. (Grand Army of the Republic, a Union association of Civil War Veterans). In 1888, the Congress of the United States made the day a national holiday called, "Memorial Day" to be celebrated on May 30. Memorial Day, was started, it is said, by a Michigan girl's act of kindness.

Who was that Michigan girl credited with starting Memorial Day?

A.   Sharon M. "Raymond" Thorp
B.   Ella "May" Wilson
C.   C. Martha Wright Griffiths

THE ANSWER IS B

It was Ella May, and her sister Josephine Willson who inspired it in 1863. Their father, the Reverend Franklin May, a Methodist Minister from Kalamazoo had joined the Union Army and was Chaplain. He was assigned to Arlington, Confederate General Robert E. Lee's home, where since he was an officer, his daughters were allowed to join him.

On April 13 1862, the anniversary of the start of the war, 8 year old Ella and 13 year old Josephine were staying at Arlington House, Robert E. Lee's home and soon America's national cemetery. They were walking through a field and picked some wild flowers. When they came across the fresh grave of a Civil War soldier, they put the flowers on the grave. They did the same thing the next day, with their mother and aunt's help. Someone noticed what they were doing and copied them; and that is how it started, with flowers form two little girls.

Little Josephine died in 1872, but Ella went on to marry and to be made an honorary member of the G.A.R.. When she died, in 1901 they say her body was wrapped in the flag before it was buried.

Sharon "Raymond" Thorp is a Michigan girl, and the author's Aunt, and the only person who has sent him a birthday greeting every year, (with a dollar most years) since he was 7 years old. Sharon was born in Caro, MI the third generation of her family born in Tuscola County.

She married the author's father's younger brother, Gerald Thorp immediately after high school. She has followed her husband's Masonic activities and always travels with him, having visited more than 40+ states and several countries in their travels in Masonry. She is the mother of Laurie and Gerald II, a grandmother and great-grandmother.

Martha Wright Griffiths, often called the Mother of the Equal Rights Amendment, was also a Michigan girl. Griffiths was elected a member of Congress from Detroit in 1954, and served till 1974. She was also a judge and the second woman to be Michigan Lt. Governor.

She was inducted into the Michigan Women's Hall of Fame in 1983 and the National Women's Hall of Fame in 1993.

Who

Did you know that saints have walked in Michigan? Michigan is not known for saints. Not saying we don't have good people, but only two official saints have set foot in the Great Lakes State. One is Pope John-Paul II, who visited Michigan in 1969, 1976 and 1987. Plus, one called "Blessed," Father Solanus Casey; who was beatified in 2017. As of the publishing of this book, Father Casey needs one more miracle to become a full Saint.

Who was the first of two Saints of the Roman Catholic Church to have set foot in Michigan?

A. Mark R. Businski
B. Alpheus Felch
C. Isaac Jogues

THE ANSWER IS C
Father Isaac Jogues, a Jesuit Priest, was born in Orleans, France in 1607. He moved to Quebec in 1636 to minister to the Huron Indian; allies of the French. In 1641 he set off to the west to minister to the Ojibwe in a place called Sault Ste. Marie, Michigan.

In 1642, Father Jogues was taken prisoner by the Mohawk Indians in New York and tortured, and after over a year as a slave he was ransomed. He went back to France for a short time but returned only to be killed by Native Americans in New York because they believed he was the cause of their crop failure and a disease that killed many.

In 1930 he, along with seven other missionaries, "the North American Martyrs" were canonized.

Alpheus Felch was not a saint, he was a politician; the fifth Governor of Michigan, serving from 1846-1847, and later a U.S. Senator from Michigan.

He was a lawyer who was born in Maine in 1804. He came to Michigan in 1833 and continued to practice law. He took part in the mustering of troops for the Toledo War in 1835. He was a State Representative, State Banking Commissioner, Michigan Supreme Court Justice, was appointed by U.S. President Franklin Pierce to the land claims commission for California.

He returned to Ann Arbor to teach Law at the University of Michigan from 1879 to 1883. He died in 1896 at the age of 91.

Mark Businski is not a Saint either, but he is an Eagle Scout! He and his wife, Bonnie, (A First Class Girl Scout, the Girl Scout's highest award) are also the parents of two Eagle Scouts, Ryan and Curtis. He is a Flint native and graduate of Michigan State University. A Scout for Life, he says; "Scouting is no club – it's a way of life." To that end he is a long time Scoutmaster and Past President of the Long Island Boy Scout Council. He is the Director of Integrated Local Solutions at CBS Radio, New York.

Who

Detroit Tigers player Miguel Cabrera won American League Most Valuable Player in 2012, and the first Triple Crown since 1967. A Triple Crown is leading the League in; RBIs, home runs and batting average.

Who was the first Tiger to win a MVP?

A. Al Kaline
B. Ty Cobb
C. Hank Greenberg

THE ANSWER IS B.
Ty Cobb was the first Detroit Tiger to win an MVP in 1901. Cobb spent 22 seasons with the Detroit Tigers, the last six as the team's player-manager, and finished his career with the Philadelphia Athletics. In 1936, Cobb received the most votes of any player on the first Baseball Hall of Fame ballot becoming the first member of the Hall of Fame. Here's what he did; .366 career batting average, batted over .400 three times, batted over .300 twenty-three

times, won 12 batting titles, including 9 in a row from 1907 to 1915. And his most amazing statistic, he stole home 54 times.

"Hammerin" Hank Greenberg played for the Tigers in the 1930s and 40s and won a couple of MVP Awards for himself, in 1935 and 1940. Greenberg was a five-time All-Star and was elected to the Hall of Fame in 1956.

"Mr. Tiger" Al Kaline went to work for the Tigers when he was 18 and still works there. He played for 22 seasons, played in 15 All Star Games, won 10 gold gloves and was elected to the Baseball Hall of Fame in 1980. He twice finished in second place in voting for Most Valuable Player. In 1955, he was second to Yogi Berra and in 1963 second to Elston Howard.

Roads have always been an issue in the Great Lakes State. The first were paths along old Native American trails, some went along ancient animal trails.

Roads became a political issue in the late 1800's when the bicycle craze hit. Bikes couldn't be ridden along wagon rutted roads! Enthusiasts began what was called the, "Good Roads Movement", a nationwide campaign for better roads. Michigan's response was to create the Michigan State Highway Department in 1905.

Who was the first Michigan State Road commissioner?

A. Michael F. Weber
B. Horatio S. Earle
C. Stevens T. Mason

THE ANSWER IS B

Horatio S. Earle, known as the "Father of Good Roads" or simply Horatio "Good Roads" Earle. He was born in Vermont 1855 and moved to Detroit in 1889 to sell farm implements. When Earle died in 1935 they named State Highway M-53, the Earle Memorial Highway.

His Michigan Historical Monument says;

In 1905, the year the State Highway Department was created, Michigan roads were quagmires of sand, mud, and clay that trapped horse-drawn vehicles and early automobiles alike. Bicycle clubs, such as the Leagues of American Wheelmen, led the effort to "reform" roads nationwide. In Michigan, the first state highway commissioner, Horatio "Good Roads" Earle (1855-1935), a bicyclist himself, vowed to conquer "the Mighty Monarch Mud." A former state senator, Earle served as state highway commissioner until 1909. Earle helped open the state to commerce and tourism. Monuments were erected in Cass City and Mackinaw City in his honor. Although appreciative, Earle stated "the monument I prize most is not measured by its height, but its length in miles".

Michael F. Weber BSME, MBA, retired after almost 40 years at General Motors as an automotive engineer. He has had many of his designs run on Michigan roads, good and bad. Michael is a friend of the author, a Distinguished Eagle Scout, the father of 3 Eagle Scouts and past President of the Water and Woods Boy Scout Council in Michigan. He is a graduate of the University of Michigan and a gifted musician who was honored to sing for President Gerald R. Ford at the 1976 Congressional Dinner in Washington, DC while a member of the UM aMaizin' Blues 'show' choir. He continues to stay very active with music at his church in Grand Blanc.

Stevens T. Mason was not an engineer, or a bicyclist, he was Michigan's first Governor. You can read about him in other parts of this book.

Hal Newhouser was a great Detroit Tigers pitcher, and Hall of Famer starting in 1939, when he was just 18 years old, through the WWII years. After his years as a player he became a Scout for the Houston Astros. He quit that job in anger after the Astros rejected one of his recommendations.

Who was the prospect the Astros rejected?

A. Derek Jeter
B. J. R. Richard
C. Joe Morgan

THE ANSWER IS A.
That's right, the Houston Astros lost out on a sure Hall of Famer Derek Jeter. Newhouser, who lived in Birmingham, Michigan, spent a lot of time in Kalamazoo watching Jeter play. He is said to have told the Astros, "I don't think any prospect is worth a million dollar bonus, if one was, it is this young man."

What happened? They were afraid Jeter would take a scholarship to the University of Michigan if they didn't give him a big enough signing bonus; so they chose Phil Nevin.

Nevin wasn't a bad pick, except when compared with Derek Jeter. Nevin spent 12 seasons in Major League Baseball, from 1995 through 2006. He played with Houston, the Tigers and six other major league teams and is a former manager of the Toledo Mud Hens.

As for the man they called Prince Hal, Newhouse never scouted again. He became a bank executive for 20 years and was inducted into the Baseball Hall of Fame at age 71 in 1992. He died later that year and is buried in Novi's Oak Hills Memorial Gardens.

There are a number of monuments on the grounds of Michigan's Capital in Lansing, but only one is a statue of a person.

Who does the only statue of a person on the Michigan Capital lawn honor?

A. Senator Lewis Cass
B. General Christopher Hamilton
C. Governor Austin Blair

THE ANSWER IS C

Governor Austin Blair, Michigan's Civil War Governor from 1861 to 1865, was born in New York in 1818. He arrived in Jackson, Michigan in 1841 and was serving in the legislature by 1846. He was a strong opponent of slavery and secession. Gov. Blair led the effort to ban capital punishment in 1846, the first government in the world to ban the death penalty. He also worked to give women and black citizens the right to vote.

He died in August of 1894, the next year the Michigan legislature appropriated $10,000 for a statue in Blair's memory. It was placed on Capitol Square where it remains today, the only statue of an actual person on the Capitol's grounds.

Lewis Cass was also a Michigan governor from 1813 to 1831. He lived from 1782 to 1866. He was a General, a Secretary of War under Andrew Jackson, Secretary of State under James Buchanan a U.S. Senator and an Ambassador to France. He ran for President in 1848.

Chris Hamilton is not a General, but he did retire as a General Supervisor from AC Spark Plug/GM. Chris is a friend of the author and a fellow Eagle Scout. He is the Executive Director of the Old Newsboys of Flint, a group who whose single purpose is to make sure no child goes without a Christmas.

He is a Turtle, ask him; and has made thousands of others Turtles too! He played in the Rose Bowl as a member of the only Purdue University football team to have won in Pasadena, California.

Michigan was a part of the new Northwest Territory when it was formed under the Northwest Ordinance in 1787. The territory included Michigan, Ohio, Indiana, Illinois, and parts of Wisconsin and Minnesota.

Who was the first Governor of the Northwest Territory?

A. Anthony "Mad Anthony" Wayne
B. Henry Dearborn
C. Arthur St. Clair

THE ANSWER IS C.

While Wayne, Dearborn and St. Clair were all Revolutionary Generals, when the Northwest Territory was created in 1787 **General Arthur St. Clair** was appointed Governor. He was President of the Continental Congress at the time and since the Constitutional Convention would soon put the Continental Congress out of business, he got the appointment.

St. Clair was born in Scotland and had been a British officer. He came to the Colonies to fight in the French & Indian War under General Jeffrey Amherst. He later resigned that commission to join the Continental Army. He was part of the Quebec invasion, took part in Washington's crossing of the Delaware River, and the Battle of Trenton.

General Henry Dearborn served in the Revolutionary War and War of 1812. Dearborn was born in New Hampshire. During the American Revolutionary War he fought at Bunker Hill, volunteered to serve under Benedict Arnold during the American expedition to Quebec, at Ticonderoga, Freeman's Farm and Saratoga. Dearborn was with George Washington's at Valley Forge and at the Battle of Monmouth. He was present when Cornwallis surrendered after the Battle of Yorktown. Dearborn, Michigan is named for him.

General Anthony Wayne, from Pennsylvania is another Revolutionary War leader. He too went with Benedict Arnold to Canada. Later, he commanded at Brandywine, Paoli and Germantown. After winter quarters at Valley Forge, he led the American attack at the Battle of Monmouth.

His nickname suggests he was wild, perhaps careless even a little crazy. The truth is that General "Mad Anthony" Wayne was brave and always found himself in the hottest part of a battle, but he got the name "Mad Anthony" because he was a hothead. He had a temper that was not easily controlled.

A woman who was born in Port Austin, Michigan in 1888 became one of the first women to lead a national government program. She taught women to grow food to fight the war effort in WWII. She graduated from the Michigan Agricultural College in 1909 with a degree in economics and taught in Lansing schools for several years.

In 1943, she was appointed National Director of the "Women's Land Army" where over 3 million American women, mostly city girls, learned to grow food for the war effort.

Who was that Port Austin woman who was an early agricultural leader?

A. Florence Hall
B. Pamela J. Payne
C. Harriett Quimby

THE ANSWER IS A.

Florence Hall was the daughter of an attorney, banker and farmer in Port Austin. She grew up on the farm and learned about farm life and growing things. She joined the Department of Agriculture in 1917. In 1943, she was named the Director of Women's Land Army. Her charge; to recruit and organize a large number of women to provide farm labor in place of the many farmers and hired hands who had joined the military or left home to take a job in a defense plant.

Hall died in 1952 at the age of sixty-four

Pamela Jane Payne is the author of "The Strange Old Light", a ghost story surrounding the Old Presque Isle Light House. She is a retired Flint, Kearsley English, Theater and Speech Teacher. She was also was a Colorado State Trooper. Pam has degrees from The University of Michigan (B.A.) and Marygrove College (M.Ed.). She now lives in Florida with her husband Jeff. They have 2 sons, 2 daughters and 13 grandchildren

Harriet Quimby was born in Manistee County, Michigan in 1875. She was the first woman to get a pilot's license in 1911, and on April 16, 1912 she became the first woman to fly across the English Channel. Most people never heard about her feat because on April 15 the RMS Titanic sank in the middle of the Atlantic becoming front page news all over the world.

Later Quimby was a theater critic in New York, and then moved to Hollywood where she wrote seven screenplays that were made into silent films directed by famous director D. W. Griffith. She even appeared in one.

On July 1, 1912, just months after her flight across the English Channel, she flew in the Third Annual Boston Aviation Meet. No one knows what happened, but her plane pitched forward, Quimby was ejected from her seat and fell to her death; she was only 37 years old.

Who

Horton Smith died in Detroit in 1963. In August of 2013, one of his old jackets was sold for a ridiculous amount of money.

Who was Horton Smith and why was his jacket so valuable?

A. Smith threw a perfect game against the 1927 Yankees "Murderers Row"
B. Smith piloted the first airplane ride by Henry Ford
C. Smith was a famous golfer who won the first Masters in Augusta

THE ANSWER IS C.

Horton Smith was an early PGA star who won the first Masters in 1934. The jacket that sold in 2013 was the green jacket from that win in Augusta. It sold for $700,000. Smith didn't actually get the jacket until 1949. That was the year they began to give out green jackets to all the winners and they gave one to every winner retroactively. In 1949, Horace Smith picked up two green jackets, for his wins in 1934 and 1936.

He accumulated 32 PGA Tour titles in total, the last of them in 1941. He played in every Masters until his death in 1963. In 1959 was elected into the Professional Golfers Association Hall of Fame. He spent his last years as the Club Pro at the Detroit Golf Club, holding that position until his death at age 55.

As singer songwriter Paul Simon wrote in his hit song "My Little Town", we remember growing up and, "pledging allegiance to the wall." He was referring to children standing and reciting the Pledge of Allegiance at school.

Did you realize we have an official pledge to the Michigan Flag? It was adopted, officially, in 1972 by the Michigan legislature. In case you have never seen it, here it is;

"I pledge allegiance to the flag of Michigan, and to the state for which it stands, two beautiful peninsulas united by a bridge of steel, where equal opportunity and justice to all is our ideal."

Who wrote the Michigan Pledge of Allegiance?"

A. Sonny Elliot
B. Robert S. Schiller
C. Harold G. Coburn

THE ANSWER IS C

Harold G. Coburn wrote the Pledge to the Michigan Flag. In one of the strange bits of history, this author has been unable to find anything on Harold Coburn, if you know anything please tell me.

Robert S. Schiller didn't write the Michigan Pledge, but has made a number of pledges. He is a native Detroiter, was a teacher for many years and worked in his family's Schiller Construction Company doing projects big and small, including work at historic Fort Wayne in Detroit.

He attended Eastern Michigan University where he was a member of the band and the band Drum Major. He has been very active in Optimists International and has served as a District Governor. He is married to Jane, has two daughters and two grandsons.

Sonny Elliot did not write the Michigan Pledge of Allegiance either, but he was a Detroit and Michigan icon. He was a much loved Detroit Weatherman, on radio and television; his weather reports combined humor and jokes with temperature and forecast

Born Marvin Schlossberg in 1920 in Detroit, he said, he got his sense of humor and the nickname Sonny from his mother. He was a B-24 pilot during WWII, and was shot down and spent 18 months in Stalag I prison camp.

After the war he returned to Detroit, earned a degree from Wayne State University and began a decade's long career in radio. He appeared on "The Lone Ranger" and "The Green Hornet" radio programs on WWJ radio. He got his start in television with a show called, "At The Zoo."

Sonny was one of the few broadcasters in the country who was on the same radio station, WWJ, non-stop for more than 60 years. Sonny Elliot passed at age 91 in 2012

This Michigan pioneer was instrumental in finding and creating public support for some of Michigan's greatest parks including; Ludington, Hartwick Pines, Wilderness, and Porcupine Mountains. She spent a lifetime as a conservationist and even has a Nature area at Michigan's Hoffmaster State Park named in her honor.

Who was the pioneer woman who helped build Michigan's park system?

A. Emma Genevieve Gillett
B. Carolyn King
C. Lori A. Tallman

THE ANSWER IS A
Emma Genevieve Gillette, she was always called Genevieve, was born on a farm near Lansing in 1898 and was among the earliest of Michigan's conservationists. She was the only woman to graduate from Michigan Agricultural College's (MSU) first landscape architecture class in 1920. She was a volunteer and was never an employee of the State of Michigan. Among the parks she had a hand in creating are; Sleeping Bear Dunes National Lakeshore, Pictured Rocks National Lakeshore, the Huron-Clinton Metroparks system, and the P. J. Hoffmaster State Park between Grand Haven and Muskegon.

The Gillette Nature Center at the Hoffmaster State Park was dedicated in her memory in 1976. She died in 1986.

Carolyn King was not a conservationist, she was a baseball player; at least she wanted to be. In 1973, 12 year old Carolyn became the first girl ever to play Little League Baseball, and ended up being the centerpiece in a landmark battle-of-the-sexes lawsuit. She had tried out for the Ypsilanti Orioles Little League team. The Little League had a rule that said no girls, but the league president allowed her to try out anyway, and she made the team.

When Little League International officials found out sued, won, and kicked her off the Orioles. But the Ypsilanti City Council said that if Carolyn couldn't play, the league couldn't use the city's fields. So, on May 10, 1973, when the local league relented and Carolyn took the field the stands were packed with fans as television crews filmed one of the biggest events in Ypsilanti's history.

While the Little League won their case officials changed their minds in 1974 and dropped its no-girls rule.

Lori A. (Button) Tallman has played some baseball, and planted a few trees, but she is an attorney in her home town of Davison, Michigan. She earned the title of Miss Davison while in High School, and since 1983 has been intimately involved in the operation of the Miss Davison Scholarship Pageant.

Who

The French traders were the first Europeans to come to Michigan, and they brought with them their Catholic religion. Priests followed shortly after to convert the Native Americans.

Who of these was a Catholic Priest born in Michigan?

A. Charles-Ange Collet
B. Gabrielle Richard
C. Robert V. Jewell

THE ANSWER IS A
Father Charles-Ange Collet, born at Fort Saint-Joseph in Niles in 1721, was the first Michigan born person to become a priest. He was the son of Claude Collet, a soldier. He was in Quebec during the siege by the British in 1759. After the siege he left Canada on a British vessel for France. Collet never returned to Canada but seemed to regret it when the French revolution broke out and he was forced to escape to England never to be heard from after 1801.

Father Gabriel Richard was born in La Ville de Saintes, France, ordained in 1790 and came to America in 1792. He arrived in Detroit in to be the assistant pastor at Ste. Anne's Church. He was the founder of the University of Michigan and became the first representative from the Michigan Territory to the U.S. House of Representatives.

Robert V. "Rob" Jewell was born in Boston, MA. Rob has called Flint home for decades and is a long time local civic advocate. He is a friend of the author, a past President of the Rotary Club of Flint and a former Assistant District Governor of Rotary International. He is a graduate of the University of Michigan-Flint. Rob is not a priest, but he does know several who serve in the Flint area.

President Abraham Lincoln is the only President of the Unite States who ever applied for and was granted a patent.

How is Michigan connected to President Lincoln's patent?

    A. He came up with the idea in Michigan

    B. He built the model in Michigan

    C. The invention was only used in Michigan

THE ANSWER IS A

Before he was elected President, Lincoln spoke all over the country. He was on a barge in the Detroit River when it got stuck on a sand bar. He was said to have thought about his days working on Mississippi River boats. The idea that came to him while stuck on the Detroit River was a way to free boats that were stuck on a sand bar. Lincoln got the patent but it was never developed or manufactured.

Who

The Medal of Honor is the United States of America's highest military honor, awarded for personal acts of valor above and beyond the call of duty. The medal is awarded by the President of the United States in the name of Congress to US military personnel only. The award was instituted during the American Civil War.

How old was the youngest Michigander to win the Medal of Honor?

    A. II years old

    B. I6 years old

    C. 20 years old

THE ANSWER IS B

16 year old George D. Sidman, from Owosso, was a Drummer Boy with the 16 Michigan Infantry, Company C. At Gaines Mills, VA, in June 1862 Sidman volunteered to carry the regimental Flag. Facing grave danger Sidman rallied the company around the colors until he was wounded. George Sidman lived till 1920 and is buried at Arlington National Cemetery. You can see his Medal of Honor at the Michigan History Museum in Lansing, Mi.

A lot of very good athletes have played for Detroit teams. Many other great athletes were born in Detroit.

Who is considered the greatest athlete born in the City of Detroit?

A. Joe Louis
B. Gordie Howe
C. Hal Newhouser

THE ANSWER IS C

This one is a bit of a trick question. All 3 of these athletes were great performers in Detroit and around the world. Plus, all of them have a strong association with Detroit, but only one was actually born in Detroit.

Hal Newhouser was born in Detroit in 1921. He was a Hall of Fame Pitcher for the Detroit Tigers. He made his Major League debut in 1939 at age 18 and won the MVP award 2 years in a row. He passed in 1998 at age 77.

"Joe Louis" Barrow, "The Brown Bomber" was one of the greatest fighters of all time and lived in Detroit for many years, but was born in Alabama in 1914. He was the world heavyweight champion from 1937 to 1949. He died in 1981 and has been remembered in Detroit with the old Joe Louis Arena, the home of the Red Wings for many years and the famous fist sculpture in downtown Detroit.

Gordie "Mr. Hockey" Howe was a star for the Red Wings for decades and remains an icon, but he was born in Floral, Saskatchewan, Canada in 1928. He played from 1946 to 1980, 26 seasons, and was an All Star 23 times. He died at age 88 in 2016.

Tool and die makers, engineers, and machinists all began with the humble arts of the blacksmith. Blacksmiths were the first to turn out metal, make machines, and learn to design metal tools. There was a blacksmith shop in every town, and they became the first garages, gas stations and repair shops.

Who is credited with turning blacksmiths into automotive engineers?

A. Henry Ford
B. Thomas Edison
C. Charles Kettering

THE ANSWER IS C

Charles Kettering is usually credited with changing what blacksmiths work on. He was a founder of Delco, and was head of research at General Motors from 1920 to 1947. Kettering had almost 200 patents, he was an early pilot and in 1908 he invented battery ignition. GMI or General Motors Institute in Flint, Mi. was renamed Kettering University in his honor.

Once upon a time he was the most famous Civil War veteran in Coldwater, Michigan. A hero who was at first denied a grave at the local cemetery.

Who was this Civil War hero and why was he denied burial at the Coldwater Cemetery?

A. Big Slim Johnson-Bank Robber
B. Old Sam-Horse
C. Captain Nathan Detroit-Pirate

THE ANSWER IS B.

Old Sam was a big beautiful draft horse that was born in Coldwater in 1849. He was trained to pull a street car from the train station to the local hotel. Old Sam was, 'drafted", really taken, into the Loomis Battery of the U.S. Army Artillery in 1861. His training around trains helped him deal with the noise and confusion of battle.

Old Sam pulled gun # 1 till the end of the war. While the average life of a horse in the artillery was 3-5 months, Old Sam made it through the entire war. He fought at Stone River and Chickamauga where he was the only horse to get his gun into firing position. Soldiers shared their hard tack with him, cared for him, and when he, and they, mustered out they took him back home to Coldwater. He was shot many times, but, Old Sam was the only one of the 200 horses that were taken with him in 1861 to survive the war.

When he died, in 1876 at age 27, his fellow soldiers wanted him buried with his Civil War mates at the Oak Grove Cemetery, but they were told no horses. They buried him there anyway in an unmarked grave where he remains to this day, the greatest Civil War Veteran of Coldwater, Michigan.

Michigan native Joseph Jenkins' name really should be remembered. His accomplishments are amazing and his legacy inspiring.

Who was Joseph Jenkins?

A. The inventor of the safety pin
B. The first African American Naval Officer
C. The first African American to win a gold medal in the Biathlon

THE ANSWER IS B

Joseph C. Jenkins, an African American Detroit native, earned an engineering degree at the University of Michigan in the 1930's. He was a road engineer for the State of Michigan. (He oversaw the construction of I-94 in Detroit), and earned a degree in Business at Wayne State University.

On April 14, 1943 Jenkins was commissioned an Ensign in the U.S. Navy, the first African American officer in history. He later was promoted to Lieutenant JG, and after the war joined the Michigan National Guard where he was commissioned a captain. Captain Jenkins life was cut short when he died from a kidney condition in 1959.

Detroit has been a center for commerce for over 3 centuries. It was the center of a worldwide fur trade, lumber trade, manufacturing trade, shipping and much more. Many fortunes have been won and lost in Detroit.

Who was the first Detroiter to become a millionaire?

A. Henry Ford
B. Eber Brock Ward
C. J. L. Hudson
D. Augustus Woodward

THE ANSWER IS B

Eber B. Ward was the first Detroit millionaire. He was born in 1811 and came to Detroit as a ten year old. He was called the "steamship king of the Great Lakes" and was known as the "first of the iron kings." He owned lumber, shipping, railroads and more. He was one of the big promoters of the Soo Locks and among the first to use it. Before that he had his schooners hauled overland to Lake Superior.

A note, Mr. Ward's photo, along with his first wife Mary's taken in about 1842, is believed the oldest photo in Michigan. That photo is at the William Clements Library in Ann Arbor.

Who of these is, perhaps, the most famous and influential journalist from Michigan?

A. Bill Bonds
B. Walter Cronkite
C. Helen Thomas

THE ANSWER IS C

Helen Thomas was the dean of the White House reporters. She was born in Detroit in 1921. Thomas was the first woman to be president of the White House Correspondents Association, the first woman to be a member of the Gridiron club and the first woman to be a bureau chief for a major new service when she was appointed Chief White House Correspondent for UPI in 1975. Helen Thomas died in Washington DC in 2013 at age 92.

Bill Bonds is also from Detroit and was a local news anchor in his home town for many years.

Walter Cronkite is a famous journalist, but is not from Michigan. He was the anchor for CBS News for 19 years, and reported from North Africa to Europe during WWII. He was born in Saint Joseph, Missouri and grew up in Texas.

WXYZ Radio in Detroit was a pioneer of broadcasting. The station first went on the air in 1925 as WGHP - named after its owner, George Harrison Phelps. A charter member of the CBS Radio Network, the station became WXYZ in 1930. In 1934, the stations was part of a group starting the new Mutual Network. A year later, WXYZ joined the NBC Blue Network, which in 1946 became ABC.

Who

Which of these shows got their start on WXYZ Radio?

A. The Lone Ranger
B. The Green Hornet
C. Sergeant Preston of the Yukon

THE ANSWER IS A, B & C

The Lone Ranger was the first, in 1933. Later the Green Hornet became a staple, and then Challenge of the Yukon, which on TV was called, Sergeant Preston of the Yukon.

Elijah Myers, of Detroit, is mostly forgotten today, but he was once famous all over America and beyond. His work still exists and is celebrated.

Who is Elijah Myers?

A. Designer of State Capital Buildings
B. Founder of a grocery chain
C. Inventor of the saxophone

THE ANSWER IS A

Elijah Myers was an architect who designed the Michigan State Capital building in 1872. He designed more state capitals than any other architect, including the Colorado State Capital and the Texas State Capital. He also designed buildings in Mexico and Brazil. Born in 1832, he moved to Detroit when he designed the state capital and stayed.

He liked the Gothic and Neo-Classical style. He also drew the Idaho Territorial Capitol, circa 1885, Central United Methodist Church, Lansing, Michigan, 1888, and Bay City City Hall, Bay City, Michigan, 1897.

Myers died in Detroit in 1909 and is buried in Woodlawn Cemetery, Detroit.

There is gold in Michigan! It is found all over the state in small amounts. Michigan's most profitable gold mine, the Ropes Mine near Ishpeming, was discovered by a man named Julius Ropes in 1881. They pulled almost $700,000 worth of gold (based on 1880 values) out of the ground before the mine closed in 1897.

Who was Julius Ropes?

A. A copper miner from Calumet
B. An Army General and geologist
C. A postmaster

THE ANSWER IS C

Julius Ropes was the Postmaster of Ishpeming, a druggist, chemist and a member of the local school board. He arrived in Ishpeming in 1867 to run a store. He discovered gold in 1881 and by 1883 had opened his mine. The mine closed in 1897, but was bought and reopened in 1901 when they found more gold among the tailings at the old mine.

The Callahan Mining Company bought the property and opened a shaft in 1983. By 1991 the mine was filled in and closed for good, the end of the only profitable gold mine in Michigan history.

Presidents of the United States have travelled all over Michigan, and many have stopped in Flint.

Who was the first sitting president to visit Flint?

A. Gerald R. Ford
B. Harry S. Truman
C. Franklin D. Roosevelt

THE ANSWER IS C

On October 15, 1936, FDR was greeted by over 150,000 people. 20,000 heard him speak at Atwood Stadium for about 10 minutes. Michigan native Gerald Ford was the first sitting President to stay overnight in Flint, and the first to arrive via Air Force One. He stayed at the Bristol Road Holiday Inn. President Truman visited Flint in September 1948 100,000 people greeted him.

The State of Michigan has buildings all over the state, from Marquette to Lansing. Named after many worthy people, these building's namesakes are people who should be remembered.

Who

Who was the Anderson House Office Building, in Lansing, named for?

A.   Arthur M. Anderson
B.   Cora Anderson
C.   Hans Jacob Andersen

THE ANSWER IS B

It's actually the Cora Anderson House Office Building in Lansing. Cora Anderson (1882-1950) of Baraga in the Upper Peninsula was the first woman elected to the Michigan State House. She was also the first Native American to serve in the Legislature. The papers called her, "The Lady of the Land." She served one term, in 1925 and 1926

The SS Arthur M. Anderson is a "Laker" cargo ship that plies the Great Lakes. She is famous for being the last ship to be in contact with the SS Edmund Fitzgerald before it sank in November 1975. Arthur Marvin Anderson was a director of U.S. Steel.

Hans Jacob Andersen, a Danish immigrant to Hudson, Wisconsin was the founder of Andersen Windows in 1903.

The key to a city is a way to honor someone who has made an impact. Usually it is awarded by City Leaders, like a Mayor. There are some who have been awarded a key to a city that might surprise. The City of Detroit has awarded many keys in its over 300 year history.

Who of these people was awarded the Key to the City of Detroit?

A.   Joseph Stalin
B.   Benito Mussolini
C.   Saddam Hussein

The answer is C; believe it or not in 1980 Detroit Mayor Coleman Young gave Iraqi President Saddam Hussein the Key to the City of Detroit for his financial support of Sacred Heart Chaldean Church. Hussein gave the church $250,000 when the church's priest sent a letter of congratulations to Hussein after his election to the presidency. Later the same priest visited Hussein in Baghdad and was given another $200,000 to pay off a debt and build a community center.

What a great idea. It happened in 1911 in Wayne County, Michigan. While driving down a road, following a milk wagon, a man noticed that the milk was leaking. The drip of the milk was making a line down the middle of the dusty River Road, in Trenton, Michigan. Then inspiration hit; why not paint a white line down the middle of the road so all drivers would know where the middle is?

Who was the person who had the idea to add a centerline down Michigan roads?

    A. David Crabill
    B. Edward Hines
    C. John T. Rich

THE ANSWER IS B

Edward N. Hines, who was born in 1870, came up with that idea for road safety and many others. Hines was a bicycle enthusiast. He was a member of the Wayne County Board of Roads from 1906 till his death in 1938, and served with another bicycle supporter named Henry Ford. This simple idea has been called one of the most important single traffic safety devices in the history of highway transportation.

Hines encouraged the construction of the first mile of concrete pavement in the world, a stretch of Woodward Avenue in Detroit. He also thought that Snow removal from public roads was a good idea. Hines was a national leader in the concept of landscaping highway rights-of-way and instrumental in movements to beautify highways by eliminating power lines and billboards.

Hines Park, along the Huron and Rouge Rivers are named for him, along with the Edward N. Hines Parkway.

John Treadway Rich was Michigan's 23rd Governor, serving from 1893 to 1897. He was born in 1841. In 1848 his parents moved his family to Elba Township, in Lapeer County. He faced a railroad strike, as well as an iron mine strike during his term. He also served as chairman of the Lapeer County board of supervisors, a State Representative, State Senator, State Treasurer and State Railroad Commissioner.

Rich is interred at Mount Hope Cemetery of Lapeer, Michigan.

Dave Crabill has a lot of inspiration, but not about putting a centerline on roads. He is a friend of the author, is a marketing implementer and owner of Eclectic Sales & Creative Marketing LLC. He is also the commissioner of an adult hockey league in the Flint area. He does: graphic design, video production, web design, direct mail, search engine marketing, social media marketing, SEO (search engine optimization), PPC (pay per click advertising) and content creation. He is yet another Turtle, just ask him.

Who

The classic children's book, "Paddle-to-the-Sea" was published in 1941. Maybe you read the story about a Native American boy, in Michigan's Upper Peninsula, who carves a small wooden Indian in a canoe and puts it in a river. The carving floats to Lake Superior, and on to Lake Huron, over the Niagara Falls and is finally found, four years later in the Atlantic Ocean.

Who was the author who used his own childhood in Michigan to tell the story of a wood carving that floated on the Great Lakes all the way to the sea, in his children's book, "Paddle-to-the-Sea"?

A. Stanley B. Blood
B. John D. Voelker
C. Holling Clancy Holling

THE ANSWER IS C

Holling Clancy Holling. Holling Clancy changed his name to Holling Clancy Hollings to honor his mother's family. He was born in Jackson County, Michigan, in 1900. He loved to draw and tell stories and worked in a number of professions that prepared him to write for kids.

He went to High School in Leslie, MI. and graduated from the Art Institute of Chicago in 1923. He was a taxidermist at the Field Museum in Chicago and worked as an anthropologist. He sailed on a Great Lakes freighter, canoed the lakes for adventure as a young man and taught art.

He wrote and illustrated many children's books, the most famous being his own "Paddle-to-the-Sea", and worked for the Disney Company as they designed Disney World. He died in 1973 and though he lived many years in California was brought home to Leslie to be buried. The Holling collection is a museum dedicated to him at the G.A.R. (Grand Army of the Republic) Hall, on Leslie's main road.

John D. Voelker was a Michigan Supreme Court Justice when he wrote the novel, "Anatomy of a Murder", under the name of Robert Traver. That book became a major motion picture. It was based on a 1952 murder case in which Voelker was the defense attorney.

Filmed in Big Bay, MI in 1959, it was directed by Otto Preminger starring; James Stewart, Lee Remick, Ben Gazzara, Eve Arden, George C. Scott and Arthur O'Connell.

Stanley Blood is a Realtor in the Flint area working for the ReMax Real Estate Team. He is a proud Graduate of the University of Michigan, worked in marketing and advertising for many years, was an instructor at the University of Michigan-Flint and would rather be standing in a river with a fly rod in hand than doing just about anything else.

"What?"

THE (even) GREATER, GREAT LAKES (What) TRIVIA QUIZ

What do the U.S. Navy Ships USS Sable and the USS Wolverine have in common?

    A. Both were WWII aircraft carriers
    B. Both sailed on the Great Lakes
    C. Both were paddle wheel steamers

THE ANSWER IS, ALL 3; A, B AND C
The Sable and Wolverine were both WWII Aircraft Carriers and paddle wheel steamers that sailed the Great Lakes during WWII to train over 18,000 pilots. Among those pilots was former President George Herbert Walker Bush who qualified on the only aircraft carriers ever to ply the Great Lakes.

Michigan is known for its parks and lakes. We have roadside parks, water parks, state parks, county parks, recreation areas; we have a lot of parks. Many are named to honor Michigan people
    Which of the following is NOT a state park?

    A. Michael D. Lysher Memorial State Park
    B. Walter J. Hayes State Park
    C. Jay McLain State Park

THE ANSWER IS, A
Michael D. Lysher does not have a park named in his honor, but he has been to a few! Michael is an honored Eagle Scout and friend of the author. He is from Davison, where he first became a musician in the 5th grade. To this day you can find Mike playing lead clarinet and baritone saxophone in big band venues and musical pit orchestras. He is a long time Journeyman Toolmaker at General Motors and is the owner of M & T Engraving. He is married to Tami and lives in Grand Blanc.

    Hayes State Park is a real park. It was named for Walter J. Hayes a banker and State Senator from Detroit. When he passed away his sister bought and donated the land to be combined with what was then Cedar Hill State Park. Both are now known as Hayes State Park in Onsted.

    McLain State Park, in the Upper Peninsula City of Hancock, is named for Jay McLain, a long time road commissioner and park trustee in Houghton County. It was named for him because he led efforts to buy property on the Canal between Houghton and Hancock. It was originally called Canal State Park, the name was changed to honor him in 1931.

What

Ray Harroun of Saginaw was an engineer from Saginaw who worked for many years at Saginaw Products Company. He is also famous as the winner of the first Indianapolis 500 in 1911. It was Harroun's only race. Harroun also changed the way we drive with an innovation he used at that first Indy 500.

What was Ray Harroun's innovation that helped him win the first Indianapolis 500?

    A. He had a windshield put in his Marmon
    B. He installed a rear view mirror
    C. He took the extra seat out of his race car

THE ANSWER IS B & C
Ray Harroun decided to change the way it had always been. Until that 1911 race there had always been a "riding mechanic" that rode in the car to watch out the back to tell the driver who was behind him. Harroun thought that the extra seat and passenger slowed him down and decided to remove it. The track officials noticed his lack of a "riding mechanic" and objected, saying it was a safety issue. So he came up with the idea of adding a rear view mirror.

So, while every other car on the track that day had two seats and a "riding mechanic", Ray Harroun had a rear view mirror, the first thought to be put on an automobile. That gave him the edge in weight and the win. By the way, when he was asked if the mirror helped he said no. It was shaking so much he couldn't see anything.

The Village of Unionville in the Thumb was incorporated on April 1, 1879 and the village council met for the first time in May.

What was the first ordinance to pass at the first meeting of the Unionville Village Council?

    A. No dancing
    B. No baseball playing in the street
    C. All men must wear hats

THE ANSWER IS B
Unionville Village Council's first action was to ban baseball playing on the street, they also passed a no livestock running at large ordinance. I guess they both clogged up the streets.

Fish get pretty big in Michigan waters. Sturgeons have been known to grow to hundreds of pounds and can reach 7-12 feet in length. But Sturgeon aren't the only fish that get to be big in Great Lakes waters. Great Lakes muskellunge can get to be large as well.

What is the record for a Great Lakes Muskellunge?

    A. 29 pounds
    B. 58 pounds
    C. 74 pounds

THE ANSWER IS B
On October 13, 2012 a man caught a 58 pound, 58 inch Muskellunge on Lake Bellaire in Michigan's Antrim County. Joseph Seeberger's catch was declared a world record by the International Committee of the Modern Day Muskellunge World Record Program.

In 2012 Charlotte, Michigan was finally successful in bringing a Dolson back home after 30 years of trying.

What or who is a Dolson?

    A. A Dolson is an automobile made by the Dolson Automotive Company.
    B. Al Dolson was a famous singer/dancer in the 1930's who grew up in Charlotte.
    C. Dolson J. Manchester from Charlotte; an author whose first book was a classic.

THE ANSWER IS A
The Dolson in this story is a 1907 Dolson automobile that was built by the Dolson Automotive Company in Charlotte, MI. The Dolson Auto Company was located in downtown Charlotte and went bankrupt shortly after this vehicle was manufactured. Community members had searched for over 30 years to find one to bring home to their community.

Carsonville, in Michigan's Thumb region, is half in Bridgehampton Township and half in Washington Township, in Sanilac County.

What was Carsonville's original name?

    A. It was always named Carsonville
    B. Halls Corners
    C. Farmers

What

THE ANSWER IS B

While all 3 have been official names for Carsonville, it was first called Halls Corners for its founder, Silas Hall who built a log store there in 1853. For some reason when a post office opened there in 1857 Halls Corners became Farmers, with Silas Hall as postmaster.

Then Arthur Carson came to town in 1864 and built his own store. In 1872 he built an even bigger store. In 1884 Carson built a grain elevator. That's when the community became Carsonville.

In the early 1990's, when the old Rochester High School was being renovated into a school district administration building, workers made an amazing discovery behind a wall.

What did workers find behind that wall at old Rochester High?

A. The largest honeybees' nest and honeycomb ever found in a building
B. Jimmy Hoffa's missing briefcase
C. A 23 foot long work of art

THE ANSWER IS C.

What workers found behind the drywall was a mural by Marvin Beerohm that depicted several local scenes. Mr. Beerohm was a W.P.A. worker who had completed the mural in 1938 as part of the Federal Art Project during the Great Depression. It had been on display until 1961 when the school was renovated and it was carefully covered up. Today it has been restored and is on display at the school administration's main meeting room.

What do the movies; "Hombre", starring Paul Newman in 1967, "3:10 to Yuma", in 1956 starring Glenn Ford, and "Get Shorty", in 1995 starring John Travolta, have in common?

A. All were written in Michigan
B. All three were filmed in Michigan
C. The lead characters were all from Michigan

THE ANSWER IS A.

All three of these famous films, and many more were written in Michigan, from the pen of Michigan author Elmore "Dutch" Leonard who died in August of 2013. Leonard's father was a GM executive who later moved his family back to Michigan in 1934. He graduated from the University of Detroit Jesuit High School in 1943 and immediately joined the Navy, where he served with the Seabees for three years in the South Pacific. His nickname, "Dutch" was gained during the war when his buddies named him after knuckle ball pitcher Dutch Leonard. He lived in Bloomfield Township, MI till he died at age 87.

Leonard was a copywriter at an advertising agency in Detroit and started by writing westerns like "3:10 to Yuma". He later wrote novels full time, at least 45 novels. He was best known as a crime writer and many of his books were turned into movies. Others include "Jackie Brown" directed by Quentin Tarantino starring Pam Grier and Samuel L. Jackson, "Valdez is Coming" starring Burt Lancaster, and the FX television series "Justified."

Old Tiger Stadium at the corner of Michigan and Trumbell saw a lot of history of the baseball variety from its opening in 1895 till it was closed in 1999. The old ball park also witnessed much football history as the Lions played there from 1937 to 1974. The greatest names in the game played there. Ty Cobb, Hank Greenberg, Al Kaline, Babe Ruth, Willie Mays, Joe DiMaggio, Nolan Ryan, Cy Young, Pete Rose, Brooks Robinson, Cal Ripken, Yogi Berra, Hank Aaron; all of the greatest roamed the field. Tiger Stadium was one of the greatest places to see a ball game ever. "The Corner" also hosted some pretty big non-baseball events.

What of the following events took place at Tiger Stadium?

A. A Joe Louis heavyweight boxing match
B. Nelson Mandela speech
C. A KISS concert

THE ANSWER IS A, B, & C
This one is a trick question. All of these events and more happened at Tiger Stadium. In 1939 Joe Louis defended his heavyweight boxing title with an 11th round knockout. The Brown Bomber beat Bob Pastor to maintain the title. World hero Nelson Mandela gave a speech to 49,000 people at the old ballpark in 1990. In 1996, hard rock band Kiss performed at Tiger Stadium in front of 39,867 fans. In the category of, "and more" Luciano Pavarotti, Placido Domingo and Jose Carrera; also known as "The Three Tenors" performed before a sellout audience at the ball park in 1999.

Michigan has some of the oldest European settlements in the U.S. Which of these is the oldest community in Michigan?

A. Detroit
B. Sault Ste. Marie
C. St. Ignace
D. Mackinac Island

THE ANSWER IS B

The oldest European settlement in Michigan is Sault Ste. Marie, founded by Father Jacques Marquette in 1668 and St. Ignace in 1671. Father Marquette, who died at age 38 near Ludington, founded both cities and also discovered the Mississippi with Louis Joliet.

Cobo Arena in Detroit was built in 1960. It could seat over 12,000 people for concerts and political events. It is now part of the new, enlarged and improved Cobo Center. Most of us know it was updated and enlarged to hold on to the North American International Auto Show after its organizers threatened to leave over poor, outdated and to small facilities.

What did not happen at Detroit's Cobo Hall over the years?

A. Martin Luther King Jr's "I have a Dream Speech"
B. Nancy Kerrigan's knee bashed
C. The Doors record a live album
D. President Barack Obama speaks to thousands

THE ANSWER IS D

President Obama is the first President of the United States not to speak at Cobo Arena since President Eisenhower. Martin Luther King Jr. gave an earlier version of the "I Have a Dream" Speech at Cobo six weeks before giving it at the march on Washington in 1963. Nancy Kerrigan was attacked in 1994 by, as we later found out, Olympic rival Tonya Harding's husband and his brother. The Doors recorded 2 live albums there.

Most people today agree that Prohibition was a miserable failure that caused the rise of the mob and organized crime. The 18th Amendment outlawed alcohol sales and consumption anywhere in the country.

What did Michigan do in 1933 to begin to end prohibition?

A. Seceded from the union till the 18th amendment was overturned.

B. Bought a distillery and sold liquor to fund the state during the Great Depression.

C. Was the first state to ratify the 21st Amendment which ended prohibition.

THE ANSWER IS C

In April 1933 a state convention met in Lansing to vote on the repeal of Prohibition. Governor William Comstock told the convention, "Prohibition didn't prohibit."

The law was always unpopular, but why was Michigan the first state to ratify the 21st Amendment?

A few possible reasons; 75% of all illegal booze in the entire country was said to have come across the Detroit River, (It was said that if you couldn't find a drink in Detroit you weren't looking very hard. In the depths of the depression many thought selling booze would be good for tax revenue and the public didn't like the overzealous way law enforcement was enforcing the law.

The law was called the, "pint for life" law, which said that anyone with as little as a pint of alcohol automatically was sentenced to life in prison if they had three previous convictions on any felony. Strangely, Michigan had been one of the earliest states to implement the law, even before the 18th Amendment went into effect.

What baseball player was known as the "Mechanical Man"?

A. Charlie Gehringer
B. Derek Jeter
C. Satchel Paige

What

THE ANSWER IS A

Charlie Gehringer played for 19 years, from 1924-1942, for the Detroit Tigers. He was elected to the Baseball Hall of Fame in 1949. Gehringer was one of the best-fielding second basemen in the history of the game. Yankees pitcher Lefty Gomez called him, the "Mechanical Man", because as his teammate Doc Cramer said: "You wind him up Opening Day and forget him."

Big rocks are often found as a mark on a map, and the McGulpin Rock in Emmet County, near the Mackinac Bridge, is a very big rock that has been an aid to navigation since ancient times. It has been observed by Europeans since at least 1749. It has also been used as another kind of marker or standard.

What has the McGulpin Rock been used to mark?

A.   Water levels
B.   Southern marker of French territory
C.   It marks the month of the year

THE ANSWER IS A

Just off shore from the McGulpin Point Lighthouse, the McGulpin Rock, over the centuries, has been used to determine the rise and fall of water levels in Lake Michigan; for Native Americans and the first French explorers. Hundreds of years ago, it was under water in the Straits. Today it is completely above water.

It was described in a letter sent back to France in 1749, by French-Canadian voyager Michel Chartier de Lotbiniere, as being; "at times high and dry and at other times completely submerged." Lotbiniere determined that the Straits of Mackinac rose and fell by as much as 8 feet.

The McGulpin Point Rock is approximately 33.8 feet in horizontal circumference and 37 feet in vertical circumference. It is about 9 feet tall. An estimate of its weight puts it around 54 tons.

Thomas Jefferson was a brilliant man. He was a farmer, philosopher, accomplished writer, legislator, scientist, wine maker, archeologist and so many other things. He was also a founding father of the U.S., the third President, founder of the University of Virginia and author of the Declaration of Independence. He was just amazing.

As a Congressman, he was well known for working very hard in committees. Though he seldom spoke, he was heard through his pen. In 1782, as a committee chairman in Congress he made up words, like Chersonesus, Metropotamia and Sylvania to complete his committee's charge.

What did Chersonesus, Metropotamia and Sylvania refer to?

   A. A law firm in Philadelphia to make sure boundaries were written properly.

   B. Three new ships for the fledgling U.S. Navy.

   C. Names of states made up from the Northwest Territory.

THE ANSWER IS C

When the U.S acquired the Northwest Territory in 1782 it was a huge wilderness. The plan was to turn the territory into 10 states and Jefferson's committee was to come up with names of states and boundary lines. The words he made up were a combination of Latin, Greek and pretend Indian words.

Most of Michigan's Lower Peninsula was to be Chersonesus, the southern part of the Lower Peninsula would be Metropotamia, and the Upper Peninsula would be called Sylvania. By the way, Jefferson also used the name Michigania but that would be used where Wisconsin is today.

Flint's Atwood Stadium was named for the Island in the Flint River it was built on: sort of. Starting in about 1917 community groups had been filling in one channel of the river with junk; it was basically a land fill. When the channel disappeared so did Atwood Island.

They also raised money for the stadium project. C.S. Mott was there, not his foundation, just Mr. Mott who was the Finance Chairman of the Stadium Committee. The goal of the committee was to, "build the largest stadium west of Harvard University."

Atwood Island was named for the pioneer lumberman, and one time Flint Mayor, William A. Atwood who had a sawmill on the island from 1866-1883. His granddaughter Miss Helen Atwood dedicated the stadium in 1929.

What was the name of Atwood Island before it was Atwood Island?

What

A. Moon Island
B. Sun Island
C. Star Island

THE ANSWER IS A

Atwood Island, just downstream from Thread Creek was first named Moon Island, for Barney Moon who had owned the Island prior to Atwood. The five acre island had been a park with a "rustic" bridge to connect it to the mainland. It was also a site of an important Native American encampment called Muscadawin

---

Alice Freeman Palmer was a teacher and college president, when women did not go to college and certainly did not become college presidents. She taught herself to read at age four. Her first job out of high school was at a private secondary school in Wisconsin. She wanted to continue on in school, but could only do it if she could find a way to help support her family.

So she took college courses and taught school. She graduated from the University of Michigan in 1876, among the first women. Then she moved her family to a rented house in Saginaw and became Principal at Saginaw High.

Later she became the first woman president of a nationally known college, Wellesley, and among the youngest college presidents at age 26.

What else is Alice Freeman Palmer remembered for?

A. She was the founder of the National Organization of Women
B. She created the American Association of University Women
C. She was the first woman to have a scholarship in her name at the University of Michigan

THE ANSWER IS B

In 1881 Professor Palmer founded the Association of Collegiate Alumnae; later the American Association of University Women. She served as its President from 1885-1887 and 1889-1890.

She died at age 47 in 1902. Her husband, George Palmer a Harvard Professor, established the Alice Freeman Professorship for a Distinguished Woman Scholar at the University of Michigan's History Department. It began funding the chair in 1957 and continues to do that to this day.

The Great Lakes has seen all kinds of ships in its day. From the first European vessel the long-lost Griffin, commanded by the French explorer Rene Robert Cavelier de la Salle, lost in 1679 to the Edmund Fitzgerald and many pleasure craft and freighters.

What may be the strangest ship ever to sail the Great Lakes?

    A. The Queen Mary
    B. An Aircraft Carrier
    C. A Sub Tender

THE ANSWER IS B

During WWII the U.S. Navy converted two coal powered ships that had been used to transport people and goods on the lakes into aircraft carriers to train pilots for service. The USS Wolverine, built in 1913, was a side paddle wheel carrier on Lake Michigan, and the USS Sable, built in 1924, which was originally a paddle wheel powered ship.

They were both based in Chicago and helped hundreds of pilots qualify for carrier service between 1942 and 1945. The biggest issue with Great Lakes carriers: lack of wind and speed. At sea the wind is stronger, and the carriers could go fast enough for the planes to take off into the wind. The Great Lakes training carriers did not have enough speed and the lakes lacked a strong enough wind for the planes to take off.

The Great Lakes; Superior, Huron, Michigan, Erie and Ontario boast thousands of miles of shoreline, some of the most beautiful shore in the world.

Which of these lakes has the longest shoreline?

    A. Superior
    B. Michigan
    C. Huron

What

THE ANSWER IS C

Lake Huron has the largest shoreline of any of the Great Lakes. That might be a surprise since we have always been taught that Lake Superior is the biggest. While Superior has the most water of all the lakes, and is said to be the largest freshwater lake on earth, it only has 2,800 miles of shoreline. Lake Huron is the champion of shoreline with over 3,827 miles.

Flint's Chevrolet Avenue was center of industry since the late 1800's. It is the site of several automotive plants that built Buicks, Mason Trucks and many Chevrolet models. It was also the site of The Whiting automobile, the Flint Wagon Works and the Begole and Fox Sawmill. The Chevy plants that dominated the site for half a century was known by locals as "Chevy in the Hole" because it was literally in the valley, or hole, of the Flint River. It was one of the sites of the Great Sit Down Strike which saw the birth of the United Auto Workers Union. When Chevrolet came to Flint, the plants to build the vehicles were built on this site, but it wasn't known as Chevrolet Avenue at that time.

What was the historic Chevrolet Avenue in Flint known as before it became Chevrolet?

A. Wilcox Street
B. Mason Way
C. Whiting Ave

THE ANSWER IS A

Before it was Chevrolet Avenue it was Wilcox Street. They changed the name to Chevrolet Avenue in 1927 because it was all Chevy on that street by then. My friend David White, a local historian and former Archivist at Kettering University, told me that Flint didn't keep records or have a system for names back then. Often DPW workers used names of their family members

There is a Mason Street in Flint, named for A.C. Mason who founded Mason Truck, with Billy Durant's Durant Motors. It later morphed into Chevy Truck.

There is also a Whiting Street in Flint, named for James H. Whiting, an auto pioneer and one of the founders of Flint Wagon Works in 1882. As President of Flint Wagon Works he convinced his partners to buy the Buick Motor Car Company in 1903 and move it to Flint.

If you've ever been to Detroit or lived there you heard the words, Chene, Beaubien, Dequindre and St. Aubin.

What do; Chene, Beaubien, Dequindre and St. Aubin all have in common?

    A.   All names of the first French families to settle in Detroit
    B.   All names of streets in Detroit
    C.   They were all members of St. Anne's Catholic Church

THE ANSWER IS A, B, AND C

The Chenes, Beaubiens, Dequindres and St. Aubins are among the first European settlers in Michigan. They came with Antione de le Mothe Cadillac to Detroit in 1701. They also have streets named for them near their homesteads and they were all members of the first church in Michigan, St. Anne's Catholic Church.

The area had already been named "le detroit" by two French Missionaries; Renee' Brehant de Galinee' and Francois Dollier de Casson. It just meant the straits, referring to the Detroit River, which is really a straight.

Dr. Joseph Loop is a founder of Port Sanilac. As the area's first physician he cared for the people in the community from 1852 till he died in 1903 at age 92. Before he got to Port Sanilac he had been a doctor in California during the gold rush.

What is odd about Dr. Loop's reason for coming to Port Sanilac?

    A.   He came to town to make his fortune as a lumberman
    B.   He was a gynecologist but treated lumberjacks
    C.   He was looking for gold and he thought he would find it in Port Sanilac

THE ANSWER IS A

When Dr. Joseph Loop came to Port Sanilac he wasn't looking for a job as a doctor. He was there to get work in the lumber industry. But they didn't need more lumbermen at the time, they needed a doctor, so, he went back to work as a physician and spent the next 53 years treating his neighbors. His home still survives. It is now the home of the Sanilac County Historic Village and Museum. The ten acre site has beautiful gardens and Victorian, Edwardian, and vintage buildings, the Barn Theater and exhibits.

What do; Stevie Wonder, Serena Williams, old time cowboy star Tim McCoy and Ray Harroun have in common?

    A. They All graduated from the University of Michigan
    B. They are all from Saginaw, Michigan
    C. They all own property on Mackinac Island

THE ANSWER IS B

Stevie Wonder, Serena Williams, Tim McCoy and Ray Harroun all were born or raised in Saginaw.

Stevie Wonder is often called the eighth Wonder of the world. Born Stevland Hardaway Judkins, in Saginaw; he signed with Motown's Tamla label at the age of eleven and became Stevie Wonder. Among his best known singles; "Superstition", "Sir Duke", "You Are the Sunshine of My Life" and "I Just Called to Say I Love You".

Serena Williams, born in 1981, is one of the greatest tennis players of all time. She holds the most Major singles, doubles, and mixed doubles titles combined amongst active players, male or female. She is the only player to have achieved a Career Golden Slam in both singles and doubles.

Tim McCoy, born in 1894 was a famous cowboy movie star of the 1930's. He was also a decorated soldier in both WWI and WWII rising to the rank of Colonel. Tim McCoy got a star on the Hollywood Walk of Fame in 1973 and was inducted into the Cowboy Hall of Fame in 1974.

Ray Harroun was born in 1879. He won the first Indianapolis 500 Mile Race on May 30, 1911.

Frankenmuth is famous for chicken dinners, Mackinac Island is all about the fudge, Detroit loves its Vernors, in Flint its Coney Islands, the Upper Peninsula loves pasties and in Battle Creek it's all about cereal.

What is Monroe's famous gastronomic delight?

    A. Snapping turtle stew
    B. Baked muskrat with creamed corn
    C. Steamed whitefish stuffed with deer sausage

THE ANSWER IS B

During what were remembered as the starving times during and just after the War of 1812, the Catholic Church was said to have given dispensation for Catholics to eat muskrat on meatless days since they lived in the water.

At the turn of the 20th Century, a new phenomenon began to rise across the State of Michigan, the interurban.

What was an interurban?

A. A train
B. A kind of circus
C. When cities shared resources

THE ANSWER IS A

An interurban is an electric train or trolley used mostly from 1900 to 1935. They moved passengers between cities or towns and were used all over the state. . After 1935, most interurbans were gone, done in by the automobile.

The year is 1854, the heart of the lumber boom and still a time for trappers to make a living. Harry Chittenden Sutton arrived in what is now Sutton's Bay in 1854 to start a business.

What business did Harry Sutton go into in Sutton's Bay?

A. Lumber
B. Fruit and jam manufacturer
C. Fuel provider

THE ANSWER IS C

In 1854, Harry Chittenden Sutton established a wooding station to provide fuel to wood-burning steamboats on Lake Michigan. The little community was first called Suttonsburg. Later it became Pleasant City when a Catholic priest filed a plat and changed the name. Father Herbstrit planned to sell the lots in his village plan to raise money to build a university. That didn't work and soon thereafter the name was changed again to Suttons Bay.

What of these historic events happened at old Tiger Stadium in Detroit?

A. Mickey Mantle hit his last home run
B. Mark McGwire hit his first home run
C. Lou Gehrig played his last game

What

THE ANSWER IS A, B, & C

Mickey Mantle hit 42 of his 536 at Tiger Stadium, including his last off of Denny McClain. According to legend, Denny grooved one to him after the Tigers had clinched the Pennant and McClain had won 31 games.

Mark McGwire hit his first 2 home runs at age 23 off of Walt Terrell in 1986.

And Lou Gehrig played his last game, number 2130, at Tiger Stadium on May 2, 1939. He never played again.

Unionville is a small town in Michigan's Thumb. That Tuscola County community celebrated its quasquicentennial in 2004.

What was Unionville first called?

A. Kramertown
B. Union City
C. Horace

THE ANSWER IS A

Marvin Kramer came to the area in 1853 and named it after himself. He took possession of the land from Private William Shaver, who received it as payment for his service in the New York Militia in the War of 1812. When the town got a post office, in 1861 it became Unionville, named for the Ohio town where the new Postmaster, Horace Marvin, was from.

Invasive species of are often thought to be dangerous.

What of these is NOT an invasive species in Michigan?

A. Sea Lamprey
B. Emerald Ash Borer
C. Garlic Mustard

THE ANSWER IS NONE

All of these are invasive species in Michigan. The Emerald Ash Borer has just about wiped out Ash trees in Michigan. The Sea Lamprey has caused terrible damage to Michigan's native fish population. By the way, a native species is defined as a species that was here before European settlement.

What

In 1836 many Michigan pioneers made mention in letters and journals of the top exports from Saginaw, the Saginaw River and Saginaw Bay.

What were those 3 exports from Saginaw in 1836?

    A. Fish
    B. Lumber
    C. Cranberries
    D. Beans
    E. Fur

THE ANSWER IS B, C, AND E
The top exports were not surprisingly; lumber, and also not very surprisingly furs. You might be a little surprised to find cranberries on the list. But cranberries were a native plant to Michigan that were domesticated and became big business in early Michigan.

What is the Piquette Plant?

    A. A Native wildflower named by Jacques Piquette
    B. The factory where Henry Ford built his first Model T's
    C. Piquette Plant, the name of an early French trapper

THE ANSWER IS B
In 1904 Henry Ford designed and built the Model T's that made him famous at the Piquette Plant in the old Milwaukee Junction area of Detroit. In 1910 he moved his operation to Highland Park. The site is now a museum with the story of Ford and the Model T featured.

They were once upon a time quite well known in Michigan. What are shoepacs?

    A. Snow drifts you can walk on
    B. Wooden shoes
    C. Foot prints in the snow
    D. Storage containers for shoes

What

THE ANSWER IS B

Shoepacs are wooden shoes that were worn by Detroiters in the early 1800's. Civil War General Orlando Wilcox, a Detroit native and West Point graduate, remembered them in his memoirs, "Shoepacs to Spurs, My 60 years of Service." Those memoirs were edited into an amazing account of General Wilcox' life called, "Forgotten Valor" by Robert Garth Scott.

Before the Detroit Lions relocated to Detroit from Ohio in 1934, there had been other pro football teams in Detroit.

What was the name of the Detroit football teams before the Lions?

A. Detroit Heralds
B. Detroit Wolverines
C. Detroit Panthers

THE ANSWER IS A, B & C

They didn't last but, before the Lions, Detroit hosted teams named the Heralds, Wolverines and Panthers.

What famous cocktail is connected with Michigan?

A. Hummer
B. Mai Tai
C. Martini

THE ANSWER IS A

The Hummer Cocktail was born in 1968 at Detroit's famous, Bayview Yacht Club. Jerome Adams came up with the famous Rum and Kahlua ice cream concoction after being prodded by customers. Adams was still working at the Bayview Yacht Club in 2014 at age 74.

There was a battle that took place in Trenton, Michigan, it was called the Battle of Monguagon.

What was the "Battle of Monguagon?

A. A cook-off between Pacific Island chefs at the local Best Western Hotel.

B. A sporting event where Mongoose are trained to fight.

C. A battle in the "War of 1812."

THE ANSWER IS C

The Battle of Monguagon, or Maguaga, (the name of the Wyandot village near Trenton where the battle took place), was an accidental victory for the Americans, during the War of 1812. It was a minor battle between about 500 American troops and 200 plus British troops, Canadian militia and Native American warriors under Tecumseh.

The accidental victory happened during the battle, August 9, 1812, when American Lt. Col. James Miller met Captain Adam Muir's British detachment. As the Americans advanced, confusion on the British side caused them to accidently sound a retreat. Col. Miller's American took the field; then Miller seems to have lost his nerve and let the British get away.

It was one of only two American victories in Michigan during the War of 1812. The other; the first "Battle of the River Raisin" took place on January 18, 1813. It was the second battle at the River Raisin that the Americans lost and where the infamous massacre took place five days later.

During the Depression, the farmers in the Upper Peninsula worked hard to eke out a living on land that had been cut over by lumbermen and left barren. Little in the way of building materials was left. Some farmers used stones and rubble, some used something called Stovewood.

What is Stovewood?

A. Wood that had been cut in short pieces to burn in a stove.

B. Stovewood is a style of stove that could be dismantled and used to build.

C. A material made in Ishpeming to build houses and barns cheaply.

THE ANSWER IS A

Stovewood, also known as cordwood, was often used during the Depression by farmers in the U.P to build barns and outbuildings. They were the leftovers from cut wood that had been sawed into short pieces and stacked to burn. They were instead stacked into walls of barns. They are still quite common in Upper Peninsula towns like Chassell, Tapiola and Pelkie.

Michigan has been home to many religions and religious communities over the years. King Strang on Beaver Island led Mormons, and there remain Amish in pockets around Michigan.

What denomination's founding is connected with Battle Creek?

A. Methodists
B. Seventh Day Adventists
C. The Baha'i Faith

THE ANSWER IS B

The Seventh day Adventists were descended from the Millerites, a group founded by Vermont farmer named William Miller, who believed that Jesus would return in 1843 to take people to heaven. It didn't happen. Mr. Miller then said it would happen in 1844. Once again it didn't happen and that resulted in what was known as, 'The Great Disappointment.'

Seventh Day Adventists still believed in a different interpretation of Miller's ideas. They came to Battle Creek in 1855, two years after an Adventist church was founded in the town. With the help of Dr. John Kellogg, an Adventist himself, they built a new headquarters and a hospital.

By 1901 the church had begun to move out of Battle Creek, its leader. Ellen White thought that the city was becoming too worldly. There was also a disagreement with Dr. Kellogg. By 1903, the church had moved to Takoma Park, Maryland. The Church continues to maintain a church heritage center in Battle Creek, a reminder of when the church was formed in the wilderness of the west.

When Michigan was first being settled, after the War of 1812 and the opening of the Erie Canal in 1825, the pioneers had to worry about a lot of things, starvation, Indian attacks, and lack of transportation. But the most common issue for those early Michiganians was "forest fever", sometimes called ague. We see these terms used constantly in articles and letters of the day.

What is forest fever or ague?

A. Malaria
B. Tainted moonshine
C. Food poisoning

THE ANSWER IS A

Forest fever or ague, is malaria, a mosquito-borne illness that was naturally found in the marshy, swampy land found in Michigan.

Alexis de Tocqueville, while visiting Michigan in 1831 asked settlers why they would subject their families to such an unhealthy environment. A Saginaw Valley pioneer answered; "Clearing land is always a dangerous business." The fact was they were looking to improve their lot in life and land, to them, was the key.

According to reports of the time almost everyone who came to Michigan before 1880 was stricken with the disease, and of all disease reported in Michigan at the time, between 50% and 75% were cases of "forest fever." After 1880, the widespread draining of the swamps finally slowed the threat of the ague.

By the way, the word "ague", comes from middle French meaning, acute, as in acute fever.

Electric automobiles are making a comeback. That's right; they have been around for over 150 years. The first electric car was built in Scotland in 1837, the first in the U.S. in 1896. By 1912, Detroit was the biggest manufacturer of gas cars in the world, and they got into electrics. One of the biggest names was Detroit Electric, which moved to Detroit from Port Huron in 1895. They were open till 1939 and manufactured over 14,000 electric vehicles. There were a number of problems with electrics, but one would be the biggest.

What was the biggest problem with the original electric cars?

A. No electricity in rural areas
B. Batteries needed too long to charge
C. They were not considered a "manly" vehicle

THE ANSWER IS C

Driving an early vehicle took a man to turn the crank to get it started. The early electrics were considered a "woman's" car because it didn't have to be cranked and a manly man wouldn't have a woman's car. When Charles Kettering invented the self-starter for gas engines in 1911, some say he brought the end of the electric. Now, nobody had to crank car to get it started so even women could drive them too.

By the way, some of the same issues from back then are haunting to-day's modern electrics; a limited range and batteries that take a long time to charge and don't last long enough.

In 1885 the Ypsilanti Underwear Company, on the Huron River, decided to become a world leader in ladies undergarments. They were at the center of the movement to stop stuffing women into Victorian garments. The long woolen underwear were less restrictive, warmer and were advocated, as part of the "Dress Reform Movement" by Jenness Miller, Amelia Bloomer, Elizabeth Caty Stanton and Dr. John Kellogg. By 1900, the dress reform movement was coming to an end. By 1907, the Ypsilanti Underwear Company was out of business.

What is said to have put the Ypsilanti Underwear Company out of business?

    A. Women were interested in fancier undergarments
    B. Wool was getting too expensive
    C. Central heating in homes

THE ANSWER IS C

There were a number of reasons for the demise of the Ypsilanti Underwear Company, but many thought that the spread of central heating in homes reduced the need for long woolen underwear for women.

Ernest Hemmingway is considered one of the great American writers. He won a Pulitzer Prize in 1953 for "The Old Man and the Sea", and the next year was awarded the Nobel Prize in Literature for the breadth of his work. "The Sun Also Rises", "A Farewell to Arms", "For Whom the Bell Tolls" are just a few.

He spent much of his youth in Michigan, at a family cottage at Walloon Lake, near Petoskey. After his death in 1961, his "Nick Adams Stories" was published. The book is a series of short stories, most of them based in Michigan. One of the stories is titled, "The Big Two Hearted River", which is a real trout stream that Hemmingway visited.

Some suggest that he was actually describing another river.

What river is described in Hemmingway's short story, "The Big Two Hearted River"?

    A. Au Sable River
    B. Pere Marquette
    C. Fox River

THE ANSWER IS C

It seems Hemmingway really liked the name, "Big Two Hearted River", and why not; it's a great name. But the description of the place in the book, according to researchers, was of the Fox River near Seney in the Upper Peninsula.

The Big Two Hearted River near Gran Marias in the U.P is about 23 miles long. Bells Brewery makes a hoppy beer using the name.

In 1940, Franklin D. Roosevelt was considering the unthinkable, running for a third term as President. It was unthinkable because George Washington himself had set an unofficial term limit by stepping down after his two terms.

His Vice President at the time, John Nance Garner, was considered a political liability and they were looking for a replacement. Michigan Senator Prentiss Brown was nominated, but declined.

What did Sen. Brown say when turning down the 1940 nomination for Vice President?

    A. "I'm tired of Washington"
    B. "That job isn't worth a warm bucket of spit"
    C. "I've experienced enough honor for one day"

THE ANSWER IS C

On the same day he was nominated for Vice President his daughter, Barbara, was crowned National Cherry Queen. When informed of his nomination his response was classic, "I've experienced enough honor for one day."

It was actually Franklin Roosevelt's Vice President John Nance who said "the office of Vice President isn't worth a bucket of warm piss." The quote was cleaned up for many years in keeping with our puritan style.

What

Hilda Mueller, of Bay City, was world famous as a boat racer. Born in 1909, she looked for something exciting to do and discovered outboard hydroplane racing. On Memorial Day, 1930; she set her first speed record at 38.52 MPH. That year she became the first woman to win a national championship. She raced for just three years and set many records. She won lots of trophies, but not much money. In 1931, she decided to try something else, and set another record.

What did Hilda Mueller do, other than race boats, in 1931?

    A.   Swam the Straights of Mackinac
    B.   Raced at Indianapolis
    C.   Set a flight record

THE ANSWER IS C

In 1931, Hilda tried her hand at flying and on May 30, 1931. She flew solo after only 4.5 hours of flight training. This feat was accomplished at the James Clements airport in Bay City. Hilda Mueller retired in 1933 from racing when she married Earl Wuepper. In three years she had set 9 world records, and won two national championship trophies.

    She died in 1978 in Gaylord.

The "Spirit of Detroit" is a marvelous 16 foot high sculpture of a kneeling giant with arms spread 22 feet. It is at the front of the Coleman Young Municipal Center in Detroit.

It is an icon of the City of Detroit and the State of Michigan and was done by American sculptor Marshall Fredericks, who was born in Rock Island, Illinois, and worked out of his primary studio in Royal Oak, Michigan.

He is famous for other sculptures that are iconic in Michigan, and around the world. He created more than 450 sculptures that grace public and private spaces all over the state. People in Flint and Detroit will remember his, "The Friendly Frog" in 1970 that was placed in malls. (Today one is at the historic "Applewood Estate" of C.S. Mott in Flint), in Port Huron they see his "Night and Day Fountain" built in 1962.

What is considered Marshall Fredericks largest commission?

A. The Thinker
B. The St. Louis Arch
C. Christ on the Cross

THE ANSWER IS C

"Christ on the Cross" is thought to be the largest wood and bronze crucifix in the world; which Fredericks considered his greatest challenge, is at Indian River, Michigan. It's also called the "National Shrine of the Cross in the Woods."

"The Thinker" was a sculpture by August Rodin and the arch was designed by famous architect Eero Saarinen.

"Tarzan of the Apes" was one of many books written by Edgar Rice Burroughs. For many years he wrote what they called 'pulp fiction." He created Tarzan and another adventurer who has been played in movies about space travel, John Carter. He does have a connection to Michigan.

What is Edgar Rice Burroughs connection to Michigan?

A. He wrote some of his stories in Michigan
B. He went to school in Michigan
C. He vacationed in Michigan

THE ANSWER IS A, B & C

Edgar Rice Burroughs was born in Chicago in 1875, son of a Civil War veteran and businessman. For 20 years he vacationed near Coldwater and is known to have written parts of "Jungle Tales of Tarzan" while looking out on Morrison Lake. He went to school at the Michigan Military Academy.

In 1919 he bought a big ranch in California that he called Tarzana. Other residents liked that name so much they changed the name of their community to Tarzana, California.

Burroughs lived in Hawaii when the Japanese attacked Pearl Harbor, and he volunteered to become the oldest war correspondent during WWII. He died in 1950.

The S.S. City of Bangor was a freighter that plied the Great Lakes. On November 30, 1926, the ship hit rocks in a blizzard off the coast of Keweenaw Point near Copper Harbor, Michigan in the Upper Peninsula and tore open the hull. The 29 sailors aboard made it to shore as their vessel practically turned into a chunk of ice. All were rescued as was the cargo.

What was the S.S. City of Bangor carrying when she hit rocks near Copper Harbor?

    A.   248 brand new cars
    B.   72 six inch cannon for the Wisconsin National Guard
    C.   Gold from the Ropes gold mine near Ishpeming

THE ANSWER IS A

The City of Bangor was carrying 248 brand new 1926 Chryslers from Detroit to Duluth, Minnesota. The wind of the storm blew 18 of the new vehicles off the deck, and they ended up washing up on the Keweenaw's shore. The rest were driven off the ship, over the ice and into Copper Harbor where they were stored till spring. Then they were driven to Calumet and loaded on a train to Detroit.

Today what's left of the ship is a site for Scuba diving.

From the Civil War came a great number of statues. Many local communities have the memorials in their town square or cemeteries. Michigan natives have had a number of statues erected in their honor including Governors Austin Blair and Lewis Cass.

What native of Michigan has more statues erected than any other?

    A.   Austin Blair
    B.   Winchester
    C.   Lewis Cass

THE ANSWER IS B

Winchester has several statues and his remains were mounted and still exist at the Smithsonian in Washington. Winchester was a famous horse ridden by General Phil Sheridan. Winchester was born on a farm in Fair Plain Township,

What

Montcalm County, MI in 1861. He served in over 50 battles, was wounded 4 times. He was assigned to Gen. Sheridan at Rienzi, Mississippi in 1862 and he named him after that town.

He got the name Winchester from a poem called "Sheridan's Ride" by Thomas Buchanan Read. It was about the Battle of Cedar Creek when Sheridan was 20 miles away when the battle started. The General jumped on Rienzi and galloped the 20 miles and saved the day. The poet called the horse Winchester, perhaps because it rhymed better than Rienzi.

There is a statue of Winchester and Gen. Sheridan at; Sheridan Circle Park in Washington DC, at Somerset, Ohio, in front of the New York State capital, and in Chicago at Lake Shore Drive and Belmont. Who would have guessed that Michigan's most recognized Civil War hero would be a horse.

Cholera was a dreaded disease in the 1800's. Its spread was fast and deadly. It was spread by contaminated water, but people didn't know that then. Perhaps the last victim of the Detroit cholera outbreak in 1832 was one of the most famous and beloved people in the frontier city.

What was this famous and beloved person known for?

A. Being a priest
B. Being a member of the U.S. Congress
C. Being a founder of the University of Michigan

THE ANSWER IS, A, B, AND C
Father Gabriel Richard, pastor of St. Anne's Catholic Church, had been the Michigan Territorial Representative to Congress and was a founder of the University of Michigan. He contracted the disease ministering and nursing victims of cholera. He died on September 12, 1832, among the last of upwards of 100 who did. Cholera would hit Detroit four more times before they realized the connection between sewage and the disease.

According to legend, on December 17, 1811, Native Americans living around Orchard Lake in what is now Oakland County reported they had a big turtle feast. They said the lake began to boil, bubble, foam and roll, as though it was a large kettle over a hot fire, and that the turtles came up in great numbers and got to shore.

What did they witness?

    A.   A visit from an ancient lake spirit
    B.   A volcanic eruption
    C.   A major earthquake

THE ANSWER IS C
They witnessed the long range effect of the New Madrid Earthquake, in New Madrid, Missouri. The quake devastated Missouri, changed the flow of rivers and even the direction, created lakes and made others disappear. It was said it made church bells in Boston ring, and in Detroit people reported feeling 9 separate tremors.

The old Bristol Road Holiday Inn, in Flint, hosted many guests and some exciting things happened there. What exciting things happened at the old Bristol Road Holiday Inn in Flint?

    A.   A President of the United States spent the night
    B.   A rock star drove a car into the pool
    C.   An alleged encounter with a U.F.O.

THE ANSWER IS A & B
In 1976, President Gerald Ford spent the night at the Bristol Road Holiday Inn in Flint. In 1966 Keith Moon, of the Who, drove his car into the pool in what has become a rock and roll legend. Perhaps he saw a U.F.O. that night, but that wasn't reported.

The largest city, by far, in Michigan is Detroit. As you drive to and from the Motor City you will cross the "Mile" roads. As a matter of fact, it is "8 Mile Road" that marks the city limits.

What the question; "8 Mile Road" in Detroit is 8 miles from what?

    A.   8 miles from the Detroit River
    B.   8 miles from Campus Martius
    C.   8 miles from Fort Wayne

THE ANSWER IS B

8 mile Road is 8 miles from Campus Martius, which is at the original center of the city. It is the hub, like the spokes of a wheel, where all the ancient Native American trails to Saginaw, Toledo, Port Huron and Grand Rapids met. Those trails are now streets called; Jefferson, Gratiot, Woodward, Grand River and Fort.

Campus Martius is where the city's first train station and city hall were built. The roads at one through six mile are not numbered, but Michigan Avenue would be zero mile.

8 Mile is more than just a road. It is the base line to set boundaries for all counties in southern Michigan. It can also be traced all the way across Lake Michigan where is close to the dividing line between Wisconsin and Illinois.

8 Mile also has a cultural significance as a sort of racial dividing line. Rapper Eminem had a song, album and award winning film called "8 Mile".

Which of these did a person from Bay City accomplish?

A. Found the source of the Mississippi
B. Fly a plane under the Mackinac Bridge
C. Ride a barrel over Niagara Falls
D. Win 2 Medals of Honor in one month

THE ANSWER IS C

On October 24, 1901, her 63rd birthday, a dance teacher from Bay City named Annie Edson Taylor, became the first person to survive a trip over Niagara Falls in a barrel. She was rowed out into the river and got in that barrel with her lucky heart shaped pillow and set adrift on the American side, near Goat Island. She went over on the Canadian side in a trip that took 20 minutes. She had a small cut on her head, otherwise unharmed.

After she got out of the barrel she said "If it was with my dying breath, I would caution anyone against attempting the feat... I would sooner walk up to the mouth of a cannon, knowing it was going to blow me to pieces than make another trip over the Fall."

Why did she do it? She wanted to make some money and not end up in the poor house.

She did make some money, but after her amazing feat her manager took the money and her barrel and disappeared. Over the years, she taught dance, music, wrote a book, worked as a clairvoyant, did magnetic therapeutic treatments and sold pictures of herself at her souvenir stand near the falls.

What

By the way, someone from Michigan did all of the accomplishments mentioned; Henry Schoolcraft found the source of the Mississippi, an Air Force plane flew under the Big Mac Bridge, and Lt. Tom Custer, George Armstrong Custer's brother, won two medals of Honor in a month during the Civil War.

Michigan's lakes have been battling invasive species for years. The Sea Lamprey has caused significant damage to the fish, and Zebra Mussels have damaged infrastructure.

Which of the following is an invasive species to Michigan?

A. Smelt
B. Muskellunge
C. Pike

THE ANSWER IS A

Smelt is an invasive species

The Great Lakes have been severely damaged by more than 180 invasive species since sea lampreys were first found after the Erie Canal opened in 1825. Since then species such as the zebra mussel and alewives have been introduced to the Great Lakes either accidently, being discharged from the ballasts of ships, or as part of a planned introduction of sport fish, such as Coho Salmon.

Smelt, officially Rainbow Smelt invaded the Great Lakes when they were introduced to Crystal Lake, in Benzie County Michigan in 1912. The lake drains into Lake Michigan so smelt spread quickly throughout the Great Lakes and their tributaries. Smelt are native to the Pacific and Atlantic coastline, where they live in both salt and fresh water.

Higgins Lake is one of the most beautiful lakes in Michigan. It is also the deepest lake that is not one of the Great Lakes in the state. It can reach depths of 135 feet. It is in Roscommon County in Northern Michigan.

What do Hillcrest, Lyon Manor, Detroit Park, Cook Corner, Sharps Corner, Almeda Beach, Oak Grove, Ritz Corner, Pine Bluffs, and Cottage Grove have to do with Higgins Lake?

What

A. Communities that make up Higgins Lake
B. They are towns tourists first came from
C. They are the names of old area lumber mills

THE ANSWER IS A

Higgins Lake is actually a small unincorporated community along the shores of Higgins Lake. The ZIP code is 48627 and it includes; Hillcrest, Lyon Manor, Detroit Park, Cook Corner, Sharps Corner, Almeda Beach, Oak Grove, Ritz Corner, Pine Bluffs, and Cottage Grove, all small communities that are situated around the lakes 21 miles of shoreline.

Houghton Lake was named in honor of Michigan's first state geologist, Douglas Houghton in 1879. He drowned in 1845 near Eagle Harbor in the Upper Peninsula while doing a survey on Lake Superior.

What was Houghton Lake known as before it became Houghton Lake?

A. Roscommon Lake
B. Big Lake
C. Lumber Lake

THE ANSWER IS A

Houghton Lake was called Roscommon Lake until it was renamed in honor of Douglas Houghton.

Houghton was a physician, explorer, scientist, geologist, professor of geology, mineralogy, and chemistry at the University of Michigan, Mayor of Detroit and more.

His remains were found the next spring and returned to Detroit, where they were buried in Elmwood Cemetery.

Besides being counties in Michigan, what do Algoma, Alpena, and Alcona have in common?

A. All are Latin words
B. All are Indian names
C. All were made up

THAN ANSWER IS C

Algoma, Alpena and Alcona were all names made up by Henry Schoolcraft, Michigan's first Indian Agent. He was also a geographer, geologist, and ethnologist, noted for his early studies of Native Americans, and for discovering the source of the Mississippi River in his 1832. They needed names for the fast growing Michigan Territory, so Schoolcraft just made them up creating names he thought sounded Indian, with a little Latin for good measure.

Other places made up by Schoolcraft; Leelanau County, Michigan after his wife's pen name of "Leelanau", Allegan, Arenac, Iosco, Kalkaska, Oscoda and Tuscola

Lake Itasca, the source lake of the Mississippi River, is another example of his faux Indian names.

The Detroit Tigers baseball team has had several nicknames.
What was the Detroit Tigers first nickname?

A. Creams
B. Wolverines
C. Tigers

THE ANSWER IS A

The team, founded in 1894 along with the Western League, was first owned by George A. Vanderbeck who boasted that the team would be the "cream" of the league, and so were called the "Detroit Creams."

They were also called the "Wolverines", but then everyone from Michigan was a Wolverine at that time. The Tigers nickname came, officially, in 1900, though they had been called that since the Detroit Free Press referred to them as the "Tigers" in a headline in 1895.

There are a lot of "large" things in Michigan, for example, Lake Superior is the largest fresh water lake in the Americas.
Which of these "largest" things are not in Michigan?

A. World's largest limestone Quarry
B. World's largest crucifix
C. World's largest manmade harbor

THE ANSWER IS C

The world's largest manmade or artificial harbor in in Jebel Ali in Dubai. Harbor Beach, in the Thumb is known for having the world's largest man-made fresh water harbor

The world's largest limestone quarry is near Roger's City, Michigan. Michigan Limestone and Chemical Company operates the limestone quarry, along the shore of Lake Huron. It was founded in 1910. Limestone is a raw material essential in industry for making steel, chemicals, and concrete. It became so large because the limestone along Lake Huron is excellent, and the lake provides easy transportation.

The world's largest crucifix is called, "The Man on the Cross" by the renowned Michigan sculptor Marshall Fredericks. It is near Indian River, Michigan. It's made of bronze 3/8" to 1/2" thick. It weighs seven tons, is twenty-eight feet tall from head to toe, and the outstretched arms span twenty-one feet.

The early days of movies featured many cowboys, Allen 'Rocky" Lane, Lash Larue, Roy Rogers and "Singing" Sandy, who was really a very young John Wayne. One of the biggest of those early movie cowboys was Tim McCoy.

Tim McCoy was born in Saginaw in 1891 and ended up making movies starting in 1926.

What did he always say was his inspiration to be a cowboy?

A. Riding cows up to the barn to be milked
B. "Buffalo" Bill Cody
C. Hiding from the sheriff

THE ANSWER IS B

Tim McCoy said in his autobiography that when "Buffalo" Bill brought his Wild West show to Saginaw in 1898, when young Tim was about 8 years old, that it was a "fantastic spectacle. And why not, the Cody Wild West Show brought in over 600 cowboys and Indians and Cossacks and horses and more.

Michigan's own Tim McCoy made dozens of films, then started his own Wild West Show and toured the country. He served in WWI as a hand grenade and bayonet instructor. In WWII he worked in the Air Corp. and rose to the rank of Colonel. He is a member of the Cowboy Hall of Fame. He died at age 86 in 1978 and is buried at Mount Olivet Cemetery in Saginaw.

"Where?"

THE (even) GREATER, GREAT LAKES (Where) TRIVIA QUIZ

On March 15, 1963, the Mississippi State University basketball team faced Loyola of Chicago in the regional semi-final game of the NCAA Tournament. Now that's not a story in itself, college basketball teams play each other all the time, but this time the Mississippi Team was breaking an unwritten law.

Mississippi teams had always refused to play integrated teams and forfeited those games due to that unwritten rule against playing Black players. But this time it wasn't to be because of a college President and coach who wouldn't allow it.

Mississippi State President Dean W. Colvard and Head Basketball Coach Babe McCarthy defied the "unwritten law" and, under threat of arrest, before the Governor of Mississippi could stop them; snuck the MSU squad out of Starkville, MS to play the game. Loyola won that game and the national championship that year.

Where was this "Game of Change" played?

A. Jenison Field House at Michigan State University
B. Chrysler Arena at the University of Michigan
C. Hillsdale College

THE ANSWER IS A

The game between Mississippi State and Loyola University was played at Jenison Fieldhouse in East Lansing. The game became known as the "Game of Change", when the coaches and players at Mississippi State refused to be held to their state's prejudices and decided to play the game.

Hillsdale College would have been a good answer since when it was founded, in 1844 by Freewill Baptists; its charter barred any discrimination based on race, religion or sex, and became an early force for the abolition of slavery. It was also only the second college in the nation to grant four-year liberal arts degrees to women.

Walter Chrysler was a railroad man, then got into the automobile industry as the leader of Buick Motors in Flint, Michigan. In 1921 Chrysler bought the ailing Maxwell Motor Company. Chrysler phased out Maxwell and created the Chrysler Corporation, in Detroit, Michigan in about 1924. Plymouth and DeSoto were also part of his auto company, and in 1928 he purchased Dodge. The same year he built the Chrysler Building in New York City.

Where was the first Chrysler dealership in Michigan located?

A. Detroit
B. Kalamazoo
C. Unionville

THE ANSWER IS C

The first Chrysler dealership, not only in Michigan but in the country and world, was signed in 1924 by Theo. K. Schmidt who owned a Dort and Chevrolet dealership on Bay Street in Unionville, in Michigan's Thumb. In 1955, when the Chrysler dealership was sold, it was the oldest Chrysler dealer in the world, at 71 years. Today Schmidt Motors still exists in Unionville, but it sells snowmobiles, mopeds and go-carts among other things.

Chicory is common in Michigan. The weed is tall and has blue flowers in the fall. Chicory was once a big cash crop for Michigan farmers (22 thousand tons were processed in 1939); used as a supplement for coffee, often to stretch a pound of coffee. The roots are taken, dried and chopped up for use in drinks.

If you have enjoyed beignets and coffee in New Orleans you had a brew that was made from 20% chicory. (In New Orleans they like a strong Chicory Coffee). Most chicory drinkers are from the Deep South, Alabama, Tennessee, Louisiana, Florida, and Texas, but many like their chicory coffee in Michigan too.

Where was the chicory capital of Michigan?

A. Detroit
B. Port Huron
C. Pinconning

THE ANSWER IS B

Port Huron was known as the chicory capital of Michigan. Michigan farmers supplied almost all of the chicory needed for the United States until 1958. That was when the tariff was lifted. Why was the tariff lifted? Before WWI there were two big chicory companies in the U.S. The U.S. seized one of them; a German owned chicory business, because it was an asset to the enemy. The other big U.S. Chicory business was the Muller Company owned by the McMorran Family in Port Huron.

Today we still see the weeds with the pretty blue flowers, and they still drink chicory coffee in the south, but Michigan farmers no longer grow chicory, on purpose. They switched to sugar beets, potatoes and grain.

One of the first signs of civilization in the wilderness was the founding of a church, a school and a library.

Where was the first library association in Michigan founded?

A. Flint
B. Detroit
C. Ann Arbor

THE ANSWER IS A
The Flint Ladies Library Association was formed in Flint in 1851. Marion Stockton, daughter of Flint founder Jacob Smith and wife of Col. Thomas Stockton was the founder and it first leader. Her association later became The Flint Public Library.

Coho Salmon are not native to Michigan waters, but they are one of the most important fish in Michigan's lakes, for sportsmen as well as the tourism industry.

Where is the so called birthplace of Great Lakes Coho Salmon?

A. Detroit
B. Sault Ste. Marie
C. Benzie County

THE ANSWER IS C
Michigan's first DNR salmon fish hatchery was built in Honor, Mi. It is the fish hatchery that started the Great Lakes salmon fishery. They had tried to introduce salmon to Michigan since the 1800's. It was 1966, when they were planted in the Platte River that it happened. The first fall spawning run, in 1967, changed Great Lakes fishing forever. This also spawned a festival in the area. Since 1968 the National Coho Salmon Festival has taken place in September.

Where

We all know that the War of 1812 ended when General Andrew Jackson's army defeated the British at New Orleans; before that; the battle of Baltimore, the burning of Washington DC, and many sea battles.

Where did the first land battle of the War of 1812 take place?

    A. Mackinac Island, Mi.
    B. Monroe, Mi.
    C. Detroit, Mi.

THE ANSWER IS A

On July 17, 1812 the first land battle of the War of 1812 took place on Mackinac Island when British forces landed at what is now called British Landing. They immediately moved inland to the high ground, now called Fort Holmes, and captured Fort Mackinac without a shot being fired.

Michigan's borders were quite contentious in the beginning. As a matter of fact Michigan was forced to wait several years to become a state because Ohio wanted Toledo. That border was settled but the episode reminds of how important set borders are. However, there is one Michigan border that is not completely set.

Where Michigan's only remaining contested border with another state?

    A. Wisconsin Border
    B. Indiana/Ohio border
    C. Toledo Strip

THE ANSWER IS A

360 square miles of land remain in dispute in the Upper Peninsula at the border with Wisconsin. You remember the history; Wisconsin lost the Upper Peninsula to Michigan in the settlement of the Toledo controversy. Plus Wisconsin lost land to Minnesota so that state could have frontage on Lake Superior. And they lost a chunk to Illinois so Chicago could have frontage on Lake Michigan.

So this time, the border dispute with Michigan in the U.P, Wisconsin said no.

It started when Captain Cram, the Army Engineer assigned to survey the area found two branches of the Montreal River. He used the eastern branch as the border in his survey. Michigan, not surprisingly argued the western branch was the proper border.

This dispute has never been officially resolved, but, the area is now recognized as Wisconsin.

The Michigan Central Train Station in Detroit stands, after 100 years, a shadow of it glorious past. It was designed by the same firm that built New York's Grand Central Station and closed in 1988. The last train out of the grand old station, January 5, 1988, was headed for Chicago.

The first train out of Michigan Central Station left the depot at 5:20PM on December 26, 1913.

Where was the first train ever out of Michigan Central Station, in Detroit, going?

A. Saginaw & Bay City
B. Chicago
C. New York

THE ANSWER IS A

The first train out of Michigan Central was bound for Saginaw and Bay City.

The station was supposed to have opened on January 4, 1914, a week later, but a fire at the old terminal the day after Christmas forced them to open early.

Drinking Tea became popular in 17th century England and in the Colonies as well. It is served hot or cold, and is said to be the second most popular drink on earth, second only to water! Tea is usually grown in warm humid climates like in Asia. It was first used in China as medicine. It is grown from seeds and cutting. It takes from 4 to 12 years for a tea plant to bear seed.

Where is the place closest to Michigan that tea is grown?

A. Bogota, Columbia,
B. Traverse City, Michigan
C. Irvine, California

Where

THE ANSWER IS B

Michigan does have a tea farm, just south of Traverse City called, "Light of Day Organic Teas". It is a lovely place to learn about tea and see how it is done.

If you're like me then you love to read those Michigan Historical Markers. When I see a sign for one I often go out of my way to find and read them. The Michigan Historical Markers mark places of historic interest all over the state, there are hundreds of them.

Where was Michigan's first historical marker placed?

A. Fort Mackinac on Mackinac Island
B. Michigan State University in East Lansing
C. Tiger Stadium in Detroit (At Michigan & Trumbell)

THE ANSWER IS B

The first Michigan Historical Marker was placed at Michigan State University in East Lansing on October 22, 1955.

In the late 1700's Robert Fulton began to experiment with steam power. By the early 1800's steam powered much of the traffic on rivers and even the oceans and Great Lakes.

Where are the oldest passenger steam ships still in existence?

A. Henry Ford Museum in Dearborn
B. On the Detroit River in Ecorse
C. On Lake Michigan in Ludington

THE ANSWER IS B

The oldest passenger steam ships known to exist are the famous Boblo boats, steamers that took people to the island amusement park in the Detroit River. The S.S. Columbia the oldest steam passenger boat still is afloat is re-fitted to be a tourist steamer on the Hudson River in New York, and the S.S. Ste. Clair, also in Ecorse is being renovated as well and can be seen in the 2014 film, "Transformers: Age of Extinction", filmed in Detroit. Both were built in the early 1900's.

Detroit's Purple Gang were mobsters of the Mafia sort, they were bootleggers, hijackers, murderers and thugs mostly from poor Jewish neighborhoods. Starting in the 1920's they ran underworld Detroit. They were done in by two things, the end of prohibition, and a series of murders that finally got authorities to act and drove them to prison, and out of town.

Where did members of the Purple Gang go after leaving Detroit at the end of Prohibition?

A. Albion, Michigan
B. Chicago, Illinois
C. Windsor, Ontario

THE ANSWER IS A

While many Purple Gang members were in prison and some were dead, several others went to hide out, in plain sight in Albion. They were known to frequent the balcony of the town's movie theater for secret meeting, and to meet at other locations in town.

The Albion DDA offers a tour brochure of the sites frequented by the notorious Purple Gang.

Where

In 1911 the first centerline was added to River Road in Trenton, Michigan becoming the first place in the world where, what some call the most important traffic safety device in the history of automobile transportation, was used. It was thought up by Edward Hines, a member of the Wayne County Road Commission. It was such a simple and great idea, to mark off lanes to separate traffic moving in opposite directions.

Where did the idea of a white line down the middle of the road come from?

A. A painting his 5 year old son drew with a white line down the middle
B. A milk wagon dribbling milk
C. A one lane bridge

THE ANSWER IS B

Edward Hines happened to be watching as a milk wagon was going down the road leaking a white trail on a dusty road. Suddenly he had this great idea and the centerline was born, here in Michigan. Hines, who died in 1938, was made a member of the Michigan Transportation Hall of Honor in 1972.

It was 1901, the new President, Theodore Roosevelt, had taken office after the assassination of William McKinley. He was an outdoorsman, hunter and even a cowboy. One of "Teddy" Roosevelt's greatest legacies is the National Parks. Conservation was, for the first time ever, front and center in national politics.

One of his first priorities was to save land. Starting in 1901 he created reserves for land; by 1905 they became national forests with over 148 million acres across the country. These were federally owned lands that he just decided to remove from the market. In 1902 Michigan got its first forest reserve.

Where was the first federal forest reserve in Michigan?

A. Upper Peninsula's Chippewa County
B. Belle Isle in Detroit
C. Roscommon and Oscoda Counties in the Lower Peninsula

THE ANSWER IS C

In 1902 land in Roscommon and Crawford Counties were withdrawn from sale and made a forest reserve. This land was sandy and the timber had been taken. The idea was to let the forest grow. Today it is the Huron Manistee National Forest.

The federal forest in Chippewa County, in the U.P. became the Marquette National Forest on Pres. Roosevelt's Proclamation in 1908. Belle Isle, in the Detroit River was a City Park for many years and is now a Michigan State Park.

Warren Avis was born in Bay City in 1915. He was an entrepreneur and founded Avis Rent a Car.

Where did his Avis Rent a Car company get its start?

A. Bay City
B. Ypsilanti
C. New Jersey

THE ANSWER IS B

The Bay City High Graduate served in the Army Air Corp in WWII. When he got back he had an idea about renting cars at airports. The idea came to him as a pilot who, after landing at airports couldn't find any transportation.

In 1946, with three vehicles, he opened his first Avis Car rental at Willow Run Airport in Ypsilanti. He sold the company in the 1950's and it is now based in New Jersey. Warren Avis died at 91 at his home in Ann Arbor, and is buried at Elm Lawn Cemetery in Bay City. He is a member of the Automotive Hall of Fame.

In the northeast Michigan City of Alpena in front of city hall, on the corner of Water Street and First Avenue, is a big cannon. It was dedicated there, in front of thousands of people, on July 4, 1912. The six inch cannon weighed in at 20,000 pounds.

Where did the cannon in front of Alpena's City Hall come from?

A. Fort McHenry in Baltimore, where the "Star Spangled Banner" flew
B. Fort Sumter, where the Confederates took the first shot of the Civil War
C. The Battleship U.S.S. Maine

Where

THE ANSWER IS C

The 20,000 pound cannon in Alpena was salvaged from the U.S.S. Maine after it blew up in Havana Harbor, Cuba in 1898; the explosion that started the Spanish American War. The saying, "Remember the Maine" was the war's battle cry. There were four ten inch guns, six 6 inch guns. The six inch cannon in Alpena fired shells that weighed 105 pounds each.

Of the four ten inch guns, two were never recovered, and two were donated to the people of Havana and are displayed at a park overlooking the bay to this day. The only gun that went to any U.S. City is the gun that stands in Alpena. There is one other six incher; it is at the Washington Navy Yard Museum in Washington DC.

There have been shows and performances in Michigan since the first Native Americans arrived after the ice sheets melted. Their stage was a great fire, and even the night sky, where they could watch as warriors and wildlife tracked across the sky. Europeans were more formal in that they had a specific place to put on a show; an opera house or theatre.

Where is the oldest theater in Michigan?

A. The Croswell Opera House in Adrian
B. The Fox Theater in Detroit
C. The Michael Kelly House
D. The Calumet Theater

THE ANSWER IS A

The Croswell Opera House in Adrian is the oldest theater in Michigan. It was built in 1866 by a local attorney named Charles Croswell, who would later be Michigan's 17th governor. Not only is it Michigan's oldest, it's the third oldest in the United States. In 1985 the "Adrian Union Hall-Croswell Opera House" was added to the national register of Historic Places.

The Fox Theatre in Detroit opened in 1928 as a flagship movie palace in the Fox Theatres chain, it was listed on the National Register of Historic Places in 1985 and was designated a National Historic Landmark in 1989.

The Calumet Theatre in the Upper Peninsula copper town of Calumet was built in 1900. Stars from Lillian Russell, John Phillip Sousa and Sarah Bernhardt to Douglas Fairbanks, Sr., Lon Chaney, Sr. and Jason Robards Sr. played there.

Michael Kelly is not a theater, but he is a fine actor who, along with his wife Kay Kelly, has graced stages from Michigan to New York. He retired from Mott Community College as Executive Director of Public Information after 18 years. He has written many articles, and appeared on or hosted, written and produced many television and radio programs.

Michael is a graduate of Notre Dame University, and has earned a Master's Degree from Wayne State University. Michael was even an official Presidential Elector in 1988.

"When?"

THE *(even)* GREATER, GREAT LAKES *(When)* TRIVIA QUIZ

Atwood Stadium in Flint holds 13,000 plus fans and has hosted high school football, U.S. Presidents, like FDR and JFK, Dinah Shore, Ready For The World, John Philip Sousa, semi pro baseball, Ted Williams, Jack Dempsey, heavyweight boxing championship matches and more since it opened in 1929.

When it was built what did the designers pattern the design after?

A.   Soldier Field Chicago
B.   The Olympic Stadium in Paris
C.   The U.S. Military Academy at West Point

THE ANSWER IS C
Osborne Engineering of Cleveland, Ohio patterned Atwood Stadium after the stadium at West Point Military Academy at West Point, New York. It was built by General Builders Company of Detroit. Today Atwood Stadium looks better than ever after restoration by Kettering University, who now own and operate the facility.

Michigan borders four of the five Great Lakes, four states and a foreign country. The borders between these states, lakes and country were set at different times in different ways; through war, Congressional action and treaties.

When was Michigan's oldest border established?

A.   1963
B.   1837
C.   1783

THE ANSWER IS C
Michigan's eastern border with Canada was set by the Treaty of Paris that ended the Revolutionary War in 1783. It specified that the border should be in the middle of Lake Huron.

Michigan is now and has always been a melting pot, a reflection of the nation, and world. Michigan has Native Americans, the French, the English, Finish, Italian, Polish, Arab, Spanish and Jewish.

When

When did the first known Jewish settler arrive in Michigan?

A. 1761
B. 1814
C. 1848

THE ANSWER IS A

It was in 1761 that a fur trader named Ezekiel Solomon arrived at Fort Michilimackinac, the site is almost under today's Mackinac Bridge. He is thought to be the first Jew in Michigan. Many more followed.

In 2015 a brand new U.S. warship was commissioned as the USS Detroit. There have been several U.S. Warships named Detroit.
    When was the first USS Detroit built?

A. 1813
B. 1923
C. 1970

THE ANSWER IS A

And the first USS Detroit wasn't even built by Americans, by the British in Canada. It was captured by the Americans at the Battle of Lake Erie on September 13, 1813. After the battle, also called the "Battle of Put-in Bay", Master Commandant Oliver Hazard Perry sent his famous message announcing the victory, "We have met the enemy and they are ours."

Camp Grayling, near Grayling in central northern Michigan, is considered one of the finest military reservations in the country and is the training center for the Michigan National Guard.
    When was Camp Grayling created?

A. 1863
B. 1898
C. 1913

84

THE ANSWER IS C
The first land for Camp Grayling, 12,920 acres, was donated by lumberman Rasmus Hanson in 1913. It was first called Camp Ferris, for Michigan's then Governor Woodbridge N. Ferris. Between 1918 and 1921 more land for artillery ranges and other activities was bought and secured or leased till the Camp today reaches to about 130,000 acres. The first troops trained there in 1914.

Michigan is the home of many people of faith; Muslim, Jewish, Mormon, Christian, Buddhist, Native American beliefs and more.

When was the first Christian religious service known to have taken place in Michigan?

A. 1641 at Sault Ste. Marie
B. 1701 at Fort Detroit
C. 1716 at Port Huron

THE ANSWER IS A
The first Christian religious service were said to have been held by two French Jesuit Priests, Isaac Jogues and Charles Raymbault in Sault Ste. Marie in 1641.

Telephones are things we carry in our pocket now. There are fewer and fewer people who are maintaining a land line for their phone service. Of course before cell phones every phone had to have a cable; that means that telephone cables had to run all over the world.

When was the first telephone cable first laid under water at the Straights of Mackinac to connect the Lower and Upper Peninsula's of Michigan?

A. 1889
B. 1907
C. 1924

THE ANSWER IS A
It was on October 25, 1889 that a submarine cable connected Michigan's Peninsulas.

Apple cider, both sweet and hard, are very popular. Fall in Michigan wouldn't be the same without visiting a cider mill and enjoying some donuts. Apples are big business in the Great Lakes State.

When was apple cider first mentioned in Michigan?

    A. 1708
    B. 1778
    C. 1822

THE ANSWER IS A

In 1708 a Frenchman by the name of Francois Clairambault d'Aigremont was sent by his government to inspect trading posts. He didn't like the cider. In a report to his superiors in France he wrote, "The cider made from the native apples is as bitter as gall." He was talking about native Michigan crab apples which would be anything but sweet.

As Michigan settlers came from all over the world and country they brought with them apple seeds that they planted in the fertile Michigan soil. By the end of the 1800's Michigan apples were a top export, and hard cider is making quite a comeback today with today's craft beer and cider movement.

In 1898 residents of Mackinac Island voted to prohibit personal motorized vehicles. To this day only special vehicles, like an ambulance and fire truck are allowed on the island, and most have never seen them operate, making it a very unique place indeed. Voters did make an exception for snowmobiles.

When did the voters of Mackinac Island vote to allow motorized snowmobiles?

    A. 1962
    B. 1972
    C. 1982

THE ANSWER IS B

Voters decided, in 1972, that snowmobiles would be allowed on the Island, since that is a very slow time of year with few visitors.

The first white centerlines on roads were placed in Michigan in 1911. It was the idea of a Wayne County Road Commissioner. Michigan was also the first state to add yellow lines to roads to indicate no-passing zones.

When were the yellow lines added to Michigan roadways indicating no-passing zones?

    A. 1913
    B. 1927
    C. 1947

THE ANSWER IS B
Michigan was not only the first state to add a white centerline to roads, Michigan also was the first to add yellow lines to the roads, to indicate no-passing zones, in 1927.

Michigan was the first English-speaking government in the world to abolish the death penalty. No person has been put to death by the State of Michigan, ever! However, there was one hanging since Michigan became a state, it was a federal execution.

When did the only execution in Michigan, since it became a state in 1837, happen?

    A. 1865
    B. 1918
    C. 1938

THE ANSWER IS C
Anthony Chebatoris was hanged for a botched bank robbery in Midland in 1937. An innocent bystander from Bay City was killed in the attempted robbery, as was Chebatoris' accomplice, who was shot by a local dentist with a deer rifle. Since it was a bank robbery, it was a federal crime, so, at dawn on July, 8 1938, Anthony Chebatoris was hanged at the Federal Correctional Institution, Milan.

When

Do you have a cat? Then you likely have some Kitty Litter or something close. It's another Michigan made and created product. Edward Lowe grew up in Cassopolis, Michigan and invented Kitty Litter for a neighbor. The cat tracked the ash she was using, because her sand was frozen. He gave her some of his invention and voila, she said it worked better than sand!

When did Ed Lowe invent his Kitty Litter?

    A. 1947
    B. 1957
    C. 1962

THE ANSWER IS A

Edward Lowe invented his Kitty Litter in 1947. He was born in 1920. Before Kitty Litter people kept their cats outside, used ash, dirt or sand as cat litter when they had to keep cats inside. He also created Tidy Cat in 1964. Mr. Lowe died in 1995 at age 75, but his Kitty Litter is still absorbing.

Hot air balloons are beautiful to see floating in the sky, they are peaceful to ride in, but can be rough in landing. They can be dangerous and still a lot of fun. They were considered so questionable in Michigan that they were outlawed in 1931. But finally the Legislature saw the glow of the torch and changed its mind.

When were hot air balloon flights legalized, again?

    A. 1935
    B. 1947
    C. 1976

THE ANSWER IS C

After being outlawed in 1931 they were once again allowed to fly in 1976. Since then there are many businesses that do flights. In Battle Creek they have a festival and on soft summer days you can sometimes hear one as its torch fires and you see it floating in the sky.

When

Nicknames, many of us grew up with nicknames. For guys named Bob, they were often Bobby, Jim was Jimmy, and people who were named for their father often became Junior. That was the name President Gerald R. Ford grew up with, he was called "Junior" most of his youth. He was named for his stepfather, Gerry Ford in Grand Rapids, Michigan. Sometimes a kid grows out of his nickname and that happened to President Ford.

When did "Junior" Ford become Jerry?

A. When he became a star football player at the University of Michigan
B. When he became a freshman in high school
C. When he became a member of Congress

THE ANSWER IS B

The late Gerald R. Ford was born Leslie Lynch King, Jr in Omaha, Nebraska in 1913. His mother divorced his biological father and married Gerald Ford of Grand Rapids. He didn't know about his "biological father until he was 17. He was always called Junior as a kid, even his football buddies called him "Junie." He once said his stepfather was a "magnificent man" and likely changed his name to honor him. We know he changed his nickname to Jerry in 1928, when he went into 9th grade at Grand Rapids South High, because his Boy Scout records record it. Gerald Ford earned the Eagle Scout badge in 1928 at 14 years old. By the way, his Mother Dorothy, who died in 1967, always called him "Junior".

In past years it was common for a funeral to take place in the parlor of the home of a family member of the deceased. Undertakers did not generally own what we know today as funeral homes. Like many people with common interests, the undertakers in Michigan created their own organization, the Undertakers Association of Michigan.

When was the Undertakers Association of Michigan founded?

A. 1880
B. 1918
C. 1942

THE ANSWER IS A

The Undertakers Association of Michigan was founded in 1880 at Jackson Michigan when 26 undertakers formed their new group.

Today it is known as the Michigan Funeral Directors Association and is the nation's oldest organization of funeral professionals. According to their website the Michigan Funeral Directors Association represents roughly 1300 funeral directors serving 650 funeral homes statewide, representing over three-quarters of all mortuary science licensees in Michigan.

Don't you love slang terms that are common in the Upper Peninsula? Downstaters are referred to as "Trolls", because they live under the Bridge, (Mackinac Bridge). They call themselves "Yoopers", a derivative of the initials U. P.

When did the Merriam-Webster Company finally include "Yooper" in its dictionary?

    A. 1913
    B. 1958
    C. 2014

THE ANSWER IS C

It took till 2014 for the dictionary publisher to include "Yooper." They added the word, according to their editor at large, because it had finally crossed from a regional world to a more general usage. Their definition of Yooper: "a native or resident of the Upper Peninsula of Michigan-used as a nickname." It says that the term was first used in about 1977.

Cities like Detroit, Flint, Lansing and Willow Run were known as the Arsenal of Democracy during WWII. The auto factories stopped producing cars and began to build, B24 Bombers at Willow run, and gun sights, airplanes and tanks in Flint, all to win the war.

When did auto production stop so the plants could switch over to making munitions?

    A. December 7, 1941
    B. February 9, 1942
    C. June 6, 1944

When

THE ANSWER IS B

Automakers stopped car production on February 9, 1942, two months after the attack on Pearl Harbor, December 7, 1941. June 6, 1944 was D-Day, when the Allies landed in France.

Names are very personal things. We generally take our last name from our father, and when a woman gets married she takes her husband's last name as her own. These days some hyphenate their last names using maiden names. Women didn't have a choice for many years, they had to take their husbands name. But some wanted to keep their maiden name. But for that to happen the law had to change.

When did it become legal for a woman to keep her last name when she got married?

    A. 1836
    B. 1920
    C. 1974

THE ANSWER IS C

It wasn't until October 2, 1974 when Michigan Attorney General Frank Kelly issued an opinion that married women can keep their maiden names. The opinion was in response to a question from the state board of nursing which wanted to know if it could issue a license in a nurse's maiden name without a court ruling.

By the way, on April 14 1980 Kelly said that a husband could assume his wife's surname.

The Detroit Public Library is the oldest and largest in Michigan. Founded on March 25, 1865 in the old Capitol High School at State and Griswold Street in Detroit, the Library had 5,000 books. When it opened it was lit by gas lamps.

When were electric lights installed at the Detroit Public Library?

    A. 1887
    B. 1901
    C. 1910

When

THE ANSWER IS A
In 1887 the main library had electric lights installed to replace the gas lights. That was one year after telephones were installed in 1886.

Camp Grayling, near Grayling includes over 146,000 acres of military training ground in Crawford, Kalkaska and Otsego counties set aside for the Michigan National Guard, and other military organizations. It is the largest National Guard training facility in the United States.
When was Camp Grayling founded?

A. 1863
B. 1913
C. 1938

THE ANSWER IS B
Camp Grayling was founded in 1913 thanks to Grayling lumber baron Rasmus Hanson. Mr. Hanson, an immigrant from Denmark, donated 13,826 acres of cut-over land in Crawford County to the state of Michigan for use as a game preserve, the first state-owned game preserve, and military reservation. The first troops arrived in 1914. Thousands of military personal are trained their every year.

It's not really surprising that the car capital of the world, Detroit, is also the place where the first automated car wash opened.
When did the first automated car wash open?

A. 1914
B. 1922
C. 1929

THE ANSWER IS A
It was only six years after Henry Ford had launched his Model T when Frank McCormick and J. W. Hinkle opened their "Automobile Laundry" on Woodward Avenue in Detroit. The way it worked? Employees would push the vehicle down the line while others would scrub it clean. The first fully automated car wash was also in the Motor City. Paul's Auto Wash" opened in 1946 on Fort Street. The vehicle was dragged down the line by a chain and the brushes and water were all done by machine.

When

"Why?"

THE *(even)* GREATER, GREAT LAKES *(Why)* TRIVIA QUIZ

While Michigan has a thriving maritime tradition, it has not always been known to provide big numbers of sailors to the U.S. Navy. During the Civil War for example there were fewer than 600 sailors from Michigan in the Navy. Still, one of the most famous names in U.S. Naval history has a big connection to Michigan.

Charles Gridley lived in Hillsdale, Michigan from the time he was three years old till he was appointed to the U.S. Naval Academy in 1860. He graduated in 1864 and served in the Navy until 1898.

Why is Charles Gridley remembered today?

A.   He was the inventor of the griddle used on naval ships.

B.   Admiral George Dewy gave him a famous order.

C.   He founded the Detroit Yacht Club.

THE ANSWER IS B

Captain Charles Vernon Gridley was the commander of, Admiral George Dewey's famous flagship the Olympia, during the Spanish American War. At the Battle of Manila Bay, on 1 May 1898, Admiral Dewy gave him one of the most famous commands in naval history, "You may fire when you are ready, Gridley," forever immortalizing the captain from Michigan.

Gridley attended Hillsdale College before going to the Naval Academy. He served in the Civil War on the sloop-of-war Oneida with Admiral David Farragut at the Battle of Mobile Bay in August 1864. After the Battle of Manila Bay he was forced to give up his command because of health issues and was sent home, after 48 years in the Navy. He died en route at Kobe Japan.

By the way, the OLYMPIA is still afloat. It is the only surviving warship of the Spanish American War and is the third oldest major U.S. naval vessel, after Constitution and Constellation. Help save her. Contact the Cruiser Olympia Historical Society, 205 Wolf St. Philadelphia, Pa. 19148.

The Castle Museum in Saginaw is a magnificent structure built in 1898. It's called the Castle because it looks like a castle in France. It was built as a post office and continued in that use till 1970. There was talk of demolition, but there was such an outcry that the building was transferred to the county to be saved.

Why does the old post office, The Castle Museum, look like a French castle?

A. It was designed by French architect Francois Beaubien
B. In the 1890's Federal buildings had to have architecture that reflected early settlers
C. It is named for early lumberman Arthur Castle who had a mansion on the site

THE ANSWER IS B

In the late 19th century the federal government had a policy of having the architecture of federal buildings reflect the heritage of their communities. So, the Post Office in Saginaw was built in the French Revival style in honor of the early French traders who traveled in the Saginaw Valley.

We all know government is always looking for ways to increase taxes, at least it seems that way. What they are really looking for is a way to increase revenue to pay for important things like, support for orphans, soldiers relief, wars and defense, road building and more.

Why not a tax on single men, a bachelor tax; has one ever been passed in Michigan?

A. It's been tried many time but couldn't get through the legislature
B. No, no one ever thought of that.
C. Yes, there has been a tax on bachelors; it's now called the "single" business tax.

THE ANSWER IS A

Proposals to tax bachelors have been introduced many times over the years in Michigan, but it has never passed. It had precedent in ancient Greek and Rome, both had taxes on bachelorhood. Most of Europe had taxes on single men at one time.

In 1837, the year Michigan became a state, a Senator Edward Ellis proposed a bill that "every Bachelor 30 years and upwards, shall be subject to an annual tax of $5." This tax would have supported, "old maids." It failed. In 1848 a petition signed by 40 people once again requested a tax on bachelors to support, "indigent females, widows and orphans." This one didn't get out of committee. A bill was introduced in in 1849, and again in 1850, neither of these bills could find a sponsor.

In 1897 the idea arose once again for a $5 tax on bachelors over 30, but another legislator threatened to introduce a bill to provide a penalty for "old maids" who refused a marriage proposal from a man, that killed the bill. Bills were introduced in 1901, 1911, and again in 1919. The goal of these bills, according to the sponsors this time was not to make money, but to encourage romance and marriage. Once again with no support the bills all died without a vote.

The last time a bill to tax bachelors was introduced in the Michigan Legislature was in 1935, in the midst of the Great Depression, but keep on the lookout for yet another attempt.

Cass City, in Tuscola County, was named for Governor Lewis Cass, as was the Cass River, Cass County and many other places. A sawmill was built on the Cass River at Cass City in 1851, farmers first arrived in 1855 and Cass City became a village in 1883.

Why do some call Cass City a baseball town?

    A.   Abner Doubleday invented Baseball at Cass City High
    B.   The first baseball stitching company was founded there
    C.   It was home to two members of the baseball Hall of Fame

THE ANSWER IS C

It was the home of two baseball Hall of Famers. Leland "Larry" McPhail and his son Lee McPhail were both elected to Baseball's Hall of Fame; the only father and son in the Hall. Larry was GM of the New York Yankees and Brooklyn Dodgers and was the man behind night baseball, and team planes.

Lee McPhail worked for the Dodgers, the Yankees and was GM of the Baltimore Orioles. As American League President from 1974 to 1984 he led baseball's expansion with the Toronto Blue Jays and the Seattle Mariners. He was acknowledged to have negotiated the end of the 1981 strike, when he stepped in for the owners.

Abner Doubleday invented the game known as baseball in Cooperstown, New York, in 1839.

There is a legend at the Oak Grove Cemetery in Coldwater about a horse that is buried in an unmarked grave. It's not marked because it is against the rules to bury an animal at the Oak Grove Cemetery.

Why is a horse buried at Coldwater's Oak Grove Cemetery?

Why

A. The horse was a war hero
B. The horse was owned by J.W. Coldwater the founder of the city.
C. It was a circus performer who died while doing a show in town

THE ANSWER IS A

The horse that legend says is buried in Coldwater's Oak Grove Cemetery was a war hero named Old Sam. He was one of the American Civil Wars' most unusual heroes. He started life in 1849 in Coldwater and pulled a street car from the train depot to the local hotel for 12 years. This work got him acclimated to the loud sounds of trains and gun fire that he would face during the war.

Old Sam joined the army in 1861, along with 200 other "war horses." He pulled Gun # 1 in the Loomis Battery and survived the battles of, Stone River: where 40 war horses died, Chickamauga: where the toll was 50 horses and Perrysville: where 33 more of his buddies fell. In the end he had been shot several times but never missed a day on duty. He was the only survivor of the 200 war horses who went in with him.

In Coldwater they took him to the old train depot and he remembered the way to the hotel! He lived out his days, marching in Memorial Day parades and attending G.A.R. Reunions in a special stall behind that hotel until 1876. At age 27 war horse Old Sam was quietly buried at Oak Grove Cemetery with full military honors by some of his human comrades.

Gun # 1 is still in Loomis Park, where Old Sam left it over a century and a half ago.

Cranberries are a nutritious fruit native to Michigan. We often see cranberries on our Thanksgiving table. They come from evergreen shrubs that are pollinated by bees and grow in bogs or swamps.

The name cranberry comes from the earliest European settlers in the new world. They thought the flower looked like a crane, so they called them cranberries. Native Americans may have given cranberries to the English settlers in Massachusetts, which would explain why they are a traditional Thanksgiving Day treat.

Cranberries were once a big crop in Michigan. In 1836 the first exports loaded onto ships in Saginaw were said to be; lumber, furs and cranberries. Today there are not as many cranberries as there once were, but there are still cranberry farms in Michigan.

Why are there fewer Michigan cranberries today than in the past?

A. Michigan drained all the swamps
B. They are very hard to grow
C. Fewer people like cranberries these days

THE ANSWER IS A
Cranberries were native to Michigan swamps, and when the swamps were drained there were fewer available to pick. The Hubbard Marsh near the Wayne and Oakland County line is an example. In 1847 a family named Hubbard planned to harvest cranberries from their swamp. They took upwards of 7,000 bushels a year, until 1925 when a major draining project was completed. Today the site of the Hubbard swamp is the site of subdivisions, schools and businesses.

Wisconsin is the leading producer of cranberries in the U.S today.

By the way, cranberries are not grown under water; they grow in damp bogs and swamps. Cranberry bogs are flooded in the fall to make them easier to harvest.

Muskrats live, mostly in the water and weigh about 4 pounds. They are native to Michigan and live in the same places that beaver might also live. Muskrats have a special place in the heart of Michigan Catholics. The church seems to say that eating muskrat on meatless Fridays and Holy Days is acceptable.

Why does the Catholic Church say it is OK to eat Muskrat on meatless days?

A. Because they live in the water so muskrat is sea food
B. It is a custom of long standing and so is acceptable
C. Muskrats are mentioned as safe food in the Bible

THE ANSWER IS B
During and after the War of 1812 there were many people who were starving in the Monroe area. The British had plundered the farms of settlers, so there wasn't much left for the American soldiers. At this time the mostly French Catholic inhabitants were trying to find any food, they needed to get permission to eat what they had on Fridays, and according to legend the priests said it was OK to eat muskrat as they live in the water, like fish. In 1987 Bishop Kenneth Povich said that the practice of eating muskrat was an, "immemorial custom", that had gone on for over a century. That made it permissible by cannon law.

Why

One of the most famous automotive sites in the world is known as the Piquette Plant in Detroit. It was built in 1904.

Why is the Piquette Plant so famous?

A. It is where Model T's were first built
B. It is where Henry Ford started the first, "moving assembly line"
C. It is the first plant made out of brick

THE ANSWER IS A
The Ford Piquette Avenue Plant is considered the birthplace of the Ford Model T. From 1904-1910, the company assembled Ford Models B, C, F, N, R, S, and T there. The first production Model T was built at Piquette in September of 1908. In 1910 Henry Ford moved production to Highland Park. That is where he introduced the moving assembly line in 1913 that changed the manufacturing world.

The Piquette Plant was sold in 1910 to Studebaker who used the facility for automobile production until 1933. A non-profit organization known as the Model T Automotive Heritage Complex owns the property and gives tours today.

By the way, the word "piquette" is a nickname for French wine of low quality.

A Flint born woman named Sophie Kurys had several nicknames that she became famous for during her career, including, "Tina Cobb."

Why was Flint's Sophie Kurys called "Tina Cobb"?

A. She created corn that would grow faster?
B. It was her professional name as a Hollywood stunt double for Olivia DeHaviland.
C. She was named for baseball's Ty Cobb because she set a record for stealing bases.

THE ANSWER IS C
Sophie Kurys, born in 1925 in Flint, was a star in the All American Girls Professional Baseball League which started during WWII and ran into the 1950's. That's the league featured in the 1992 movie, "A League of Their Own." In 1946 she set a record with 201 stolen bases on 203 attempts in 113 games. Kurys, the "Tina Cobb" of girl's baseball was also known as the "Flint Flash." She racked up over 1,000 stolen bases in her career playing for the Racine, (Wis.) Belles from 1944-1952. She was inducted into the Flint Area Sports Hall of Fame in 1986 and died in February 2013.

Why

One of the most famous sons of Michigan is Jacob Howard. Even though you may not know who he is, what he did in his life affects us to this day, and you should know who he is.

Why should every Michigander know who Jacob Howard is?

A. He discovered Michigan
B. He wrote 3 amendments to the U.S. Constitution
C. He invented the lumbermill

THE ANSWER IS B

U.S. Senator Jacob Howard of Michigan wrote and shepherded through Congress the 13th, 14th and 15th Amendment to the Constitution. Howard was city attorney of Detroit in 1834 and a member of the Michigan State House in 1838, Michigan Attorney General from 1855-1861. He was elected as a Whig to the U.S. House of Representatives in 1840. He helped draw up the platform of the first Republican Party convention held, "under the oaks" in Jackson, Michigan in 1854. Howard was elected as a Republican to the U.S. Senate in 1861 and served from January 1862 to March 1871.

The 13th Amendment abolished slavery

The 14th Amendment defined what a citizen is

The 15th Amendment prohibits governments from denying a citizen the right to vote based on that citizen's "race, color, or previous condition of servitude"

Mr. Buick is now in downtown Flint, so is Mr. Chevrolet and Mr. Dort, and Mr. Durant. All put there by the people who brought us the "Back to the Bricks" Car Cruise. Now they have added yet another auto pioneer statue to the many iconic statues around town. Walter Chrysler's statue now graces Bishop International Airport.

Why is Walter Chrysler in Flint?

A. They found an unused statue of him and bought it at a great price
B. He was born in Flint and served as Mayor
C. He came to Flint to work for Billy Durant at Buick

THE ANSWER IS C

Walter Chrysler was born in Kansas and came to Flint to be President of Buick Motor Company. He learned the business from Billy Durant, the founder of GM and Buick and Chevrolet in Flint. Then Chrysler founded his own company, a little business called Chrysler Motors.

The Back to the Bricks Car Cruise has been a great party for Flint. They have used profits to build statues to auto pioneers such as David Buick, Louis Chevrolet, J. Dallas Dort, and William C. "Billy" Durant and Charles Stewart Mott. The Walter Chrysler statue is displayed at Bishop International Airport.

At the tip of Michigan there is a big bridge, a fort, a couple of lighthouses and a big rock. The bridge is the famous Mackinac Bridge, the fort the famous Fort Michilimackinac, and that big rock is pretty famous too.

Why is the big rock at the tip of Michigan famous?

A. It has long been a measuring tool
B. The rock was put there by aliens
C. It was the rock that sank the Edmund Fitzgerald

THE ANSWER IS A

The big rock is the McGulpin Point Rock, just off shore from the McGulpin Point Lighthouse. It is famous as an ancient measuring tool. A 1749 letter from a French Priest to France describes the McGulpin Point Rock as, "At times high and dry and at other times completely covered" The letter goes on to say that the straights of Mackinac rise and fall up to 8 feet.

The first Huron County fair was held in 1869. In 1881 the Huron County Agricultural Society moved the fair to what is now the Bad Axe City Park. They built brand new exhibit buildings and areas for meetings and spent a lot of money and time preparing, then they canceled the fair.

Why was the Huron County Fair canceled in 1881, the first year at the brand new location?

A. They didn't feel like having it
B. Fire burned all the new buildings
C. A measles epidemic

THE ANSWER IS B
The Great Thumb Fire of 1881 burned all of the new buildings at the site before they were ever used. They did rebuild and the fair went on as scheduled in 1882.

Studies have shown that there are fewer perch in the Saginaw Bay, and the number is dropping.

Why is the perch population in Saginaw Bay falling?

A. Because there are more walleye and fewer alewives and herring
B. Because of pollution
C. They moved to Thunder Bay

THE ANSWER IS A
When there are fewer alewives and lake herring the walleye have to eat something else, and that something else is, perch.

From about 1910 till his death in 1938 Frank White was perhaps the most famous man in Leslie, Michigan. The fact that he was a black man just added to the surprise.

Why is Frank White remembered?

A. He was the last known slave that belonged to Robert E. Lee
B. He was the face on boxes of Cream of Wheat cereal
C. He invented Peanut Butter

THE ANSWER IS B
Frank L. White was and is the face on Cream of Wheat Cereal. He was born in Barbados in 1867, came to the U.S. in 1875 and lived for many years in Leslie. He was famous as a Master Chef in Chicago when he was photographed for the cereal box. ,

Why

White died in 1938, and is buried at Woodlawn Cemetery in Leslie. It wasn't until 2007, that his grave, which had been marked with a blank concrete marker, was replaced with a granite gravestone with his image from the box of Cream of Wheat.

George Washington Carver, inventor, scientist and botanist who was born a slave in around 1864 created dozens of uses for peanuts, including inventing peanut butter.

In 1931 the U.S Coast Guard buildings at Sleeping Bear Point on Lake Michigan, located in what is now the Sleeping Bear Dunes National Lakeshore, had to be removed and taken to Glen Haven.

Why did the Coast Guard move those buildings away from Sleeping Bear Point?

    A.   Creeping Sand Dunes
    B.   Creepy place-it was haunted
    C.   Rising Lake Michigan water

THE ANSWER IS A
The Coast Guard realized that if they stayed at Sleeping Bear Point the station would soon be buried by creeping sand dunes. The dunes have taken small towns, forests and farms over the years, pushed by wind.

Why was Flint resident Hiram Smith known as "Hardwood"?

    A.   He was a boxer whose chin was said to be hard as oak
    B.   He had a reputation as a hard headed old wood head
    C.   He was a lumberman whose specialty was producing hard wood

THE ANSWER IS C
Hiram "Hardwood" Smith of Flint sold hard wood, like oak. His mill was a major producer of hardwood in Michigan in the 1870's and 1880's. His home still stands on a side street in Flint, surrounded by businesses and subdivisions.

The Coast Guard Cutter Mackinaw, WAGB-83, was retired from service on the Great Lakes in 2006. Known as the "Queen of the Lakes" the Mackinaw was said to have played a big role in the allied victory in WWII. The cutter's retirement home is almost as historic as the ship itself.

Why is the Mackinaw's retirement home as historic as the ship?

A. The Mackinaw is part of an underwater shipwreck park
B. It is docked at the site of a famous ferry dock
C. It was dismantled and taken to the Henry Ford Museum

THE ANSWER IS B

The icebreaker Mackinaw Maritime Museum Society now owns and operates the Mackinaw as a ship museum. It is docked at the famous Chief Wawatam dock in Mackinaw City. It was from that place that the ferry used to take train cars and automobiles across the straights of Mackinac to the Upper Peninsula. It was built as part of the war effort during World War II to keep war material moving during the winter months.

Alexis de Tocqueville became famous as the author of "Democracy in America." He was a minor French aristocrat who came to the U.S. in 1831, at only 25 years of age. "Democracy in America" published after his travels in the United States, is considered an early and classic work of sociology and political science.

Why did Alexis de Tocqueville come to America in 1831?

A. To hide out from the French revolution
B. To study American prisons
C. To find a wife

THE ANSWER IS A AND B

As a nobleman he was among the people who were being murdered during the French Revolution's Reign of Terror which saw the streets of Paris run red with blood from hundreds put to death on the guillotine. So he needed to get out of the country. His excuse, he got permission from the government to go to America to investigate prisons and penitentiaries and write a report.

In 1831, he headed to the new world with his friend Gustave de Beaumont. While Tocqueville did visit some prisons, he mostly traveled widely in

America and took extensive notes. There is a famous story about his visit to Flint and Saginaw, but you'll need to look at my first book, the "Great, Great Lakes Trivia Test" for that.

Why is Archibald Jones infamous in Northwestern Michigan?

    A. He was a Robin Hood figure who stole from rich lumbermen and gave to the poor

    B. He almost drained a lake

    C. He named Arch rock, on Mackinac Island, for himself.

THE ANSWER IS B

Archibald Jones is famous, or infamous for being the man who pulled the plug on Crystal Lake in Benzie County. In 1873, Jones founded the Benzie County River Improvement Company; the idea was to get a channel between Crystal Lake and the Betsie River. He began to dredge a channel between the Betsie River and Crystal Lake, but something went terribly wrong. In the early morning hours of Aug. 23, 1873, ten days after he began to dig, a storm blew up on Lake Michigan. High waves demolished the temporary dam he had put up and water began gushing through the outlet.

    The lake dropped six inches of depth by 9 a.m. and 11 feet by the next day with the flow continuing, if slowing. In the end Crystal Lake's level dropped 15+ feet in a day. But the lake didn't disappear. In 1911 the first concrete dam went in; reinforcing and protecting the lake.

    There was some surprisingly good news out of this; while Archibald Jones pulled the plug on Crystal Lake, the drop in water level revealed sand beaches all the way around the lake. Over the first three weeks of the 1873 incident, a quarter mile of sandy beaches surfaced. Mr. Jones in his great mistake had actually created what is today one of Michigan's most beautiful areas and lake shore.

Canada shares more borders with Michigan than with any other state. The treaty that set the border, the 1783 Treaty of Paris, specified that the border be "located in the middle of the lakes."

    Why did they say the border had to go through the middle of Lakes Huron and Superior?

A. The Americans lost a coin flip
B. So no one could ever find the real border
C. So each country could use their half of the lake

THE ANSWER IS C

The border set in the Treaty of Paris in 1783, down the middle of Lake Huron as well as Superior so each country could "preserve vital avenues of transportation."

Auto Pioneer Henry Ford is famous for the amazing raise he gave his employees in 1914. He paid them $5 a day, an exorbitant amount at the time. It is said he paid that much so that his employees could buy the vehicles they made. But that wasn't the only reason.

Why did Henry Ford pay his employees $5 a day?

A. So people would come to work
B. To cut employee turnover
C. Because his Pastor said it would be the right thing to do

THE ANSWER IS A AND B

Not only did paying his employees $5 a day make them able to buy a vehicle, it cut absenteeism by 90% practically overnight and it made his employees stay with him instead of moving on. In 1913 Ford had to replace 53,000 employees who quit, by 1915 that number was reduced to 2,000.

Henry Ford was quoted as saying, that $5 a day was, "the greatest cost cutting move I ever made."

Thomas Palmer was a well-known business political leader from Detroit 19th Century. He is one of the most important Michigan citizens you've never heard of.

Why is Thomas Palmer remembered?

A. Serving as a US Senator from Michigan who advocated for women's suffrage
B. Donating land in Detroit
C. Founding the Michigan Humane Society
D. President of the Chicago World's Fair

THE ANSWER IS A, B, C, AND D

Senator Thomas Witherell Palmer is one of Detroit's most important figures. He served in the Michigan Senate, as well as the U.S. Senate from 1883-1889. He pushed for women's right to vote and is said to have coined the phrase "Equal rights for all, special privileges to none."

In 1897, Palmer donated 140 acres along Woodward Avenue in Detroit to create Palmer Park. The area includes Palmer Woods, one of Detroit's most elegant neighborhoods, including homes designed by Frank Lloyd Wright and Albert Kahn.

Sen. Palmer was the first president of what is now known as the Michigan Humane Society. He was also one of the founders and the first president of the Detroit Museum of Art; now known as the Detroit Institute of Arts. The DIA stands on the site of Palmer's former home.

He died in Detroit in 1913, at age 83 and is interred in Elmwood Cemetery.

In 1934 the Detroit Lions started the season 10 and 0. It was their first year in Detroit, and the depression kept the fans away, as Detroit was a baseball town. Lion's owner George Richards, a radio executive, convinced the defending champion Chicago Bears to come to Detroit to play the Lions on Thanksgiving Day.

Why is that game remembered today?

A. It was the first time an NFL football game was broadcast nationally

B. It was the first time an NFL game was played on Thanksgiving.

C. Chicago fullback Bronco Nagurski scored 5 touchdowns.

THE ANSWER IS A AND B

The Thanksgiving Day game in 1934 was the first time an NFL game was broadcast coast to coast. It was carried on 94 NBC radio stations. 26,000 fans were lucky to get into the University of Detroit Stadium to see the game. Thousands were turned away.

It was also the first time an NFL game was played on Thanksgiving Day. By the way, the Lions lost to the Bears 19-16.

The Knights of Pythias was thought up by a man named Justus Rathbone in Michigan's Upper Peninsula. He came from New York and decided to go to Michigan's Keweenaw Peninsula for his health in 1857, when he was just 18. He taught school at Eagle Harbor and in his spare time wrote the rituals that he would use in his new organization, the Knights of Pythias. His group was about peace. He went back east in 1861, but his ideas were still there and in 1864 the group was officially founded in Washington D.C. It was the first fraternal organization ever chartered by the Congress of the United States.

Why is the Knights of Pythias the first fraternal organization to be chartered by Congress?

A. Because of a suggestion by President Abraham Lincoln
B. Because Justus Rathbone became a U.S. Senator
C. It was the only way they could copyright their official hats

THE ANSWER IS A

It was Abraham Lincoln who suggested that they apply to Congress for a charter to, "reunite our brethren of the North and South." More than 3 million people have been members, about 200,000 in 2014.

The schoolhouse where he taught and wrote his rituals still stands in Eagle Harbor as a monument to Rathbone and the Knights of Pythias.

Captain Dan Seavey, also known as 'Roaring Dan" was famous on the Lake Michigan. He was born in Maine, in 1865, where his father was a sea captain and went to sea at age 13. He was a deputy marshal for the Bureau of Indian Affairs, and was in the U.S. Navy for three years.

Why was Captain "Roaring Dan" Seavey famous?

A. He discovered gold in the Upper Peninsula
B. He was a great singer with a powerful voice
C. He was the only pirate on the Great Lakes

THE ANSWER IS C

Captain Dan "Roaring Dan" Seavey was a 6 foot 4 inch 250 pound tough guy who sailed Lake Michigan smuggling, poaching, bootlegging, prizefighting assaulting, pimping, stealing ships and committing arson; a regular pirate.

He often denied he was a pirate, but in private was known to change his story a bit. In his later years "Roaring Dan" became a Christian often seen carrying a Bible. He died in 1949 in a nursing home in Peshtigo, Wisconsin.

Being rich and beautiful is enough to make you famous today. But being famous for being famous is nothing new. Clara Ward, who was born in 1873 in Detroit, was such a woman. She was as famous in her day as the Kardashians are today from about 1890 to 1916.

Why was Clara Ward famous?

A. Posing for risqué postcards
B. Being an official Princess
C. Being one of the richest women in Michigan

THE ANSWER IS A, B & C

Clara Ward was the daughter of Eber Brock Ward, Detroit's first millionaire known as the "steamship king of the Great Lakes", and his second wife. He died when Clara was but two years old, so she became a wealthy young woman.

Clara was known for being beautiful, rich and famous. She was an American Princess, then became one literally. In 1890 she married Marie Joseph Anatole Pierre Alphonse de Riquet, Prince de Caraman-Chimay of Belgium, whose family though noble was in need of money and became Princesse de Caraman-Chimay, a real live Princess from Detroit.

The story gets stranger as she later ran off with a Hungarian gypsy creating quite the scandal. She posed for postcards in skin tight flesh colored costumes in France and danced in nightclubs. A character, played by Shirley McLaine in the film musical, "Can Can" is said to, at least in part, portray Princess Clara of Caraman-Chimay. Another note, French artist Henri de Toulouse-Lautrec painted her, and her Gypsy Husband's image in a painting called, "Idylle Princiere"

She married four times and died in 1916 at age 43.

Edna Ferber was born in Kalamazoo in 1885. She is almost forgotten in her home state but we all have heard of her work.

Why is Edna Ferber a name that should be remembered?

A. She was a Pulitzer prize winning writer
B. She stared on Broadway in "Showboat"
C. She was the first woman to serve in the Cabinet of a President

THE ANSWER IS A

Kalamazoo's Edna Ferber was a famous writer. She wrote "Saratoga Trunk", which was made into a movie, "Giant", with Rock Hudson, Elizabeth Taylor and James Dean. She didn't star in "Showboat, she wrote it! Later Jerome Kern and Oscar Hammerstein turned it into a major Broadway musical. She died in 1968 at the age of 82.

You have probably never heard of him, but, Prentiss Brown should be on everyone's list of great Michiganians.

Why Should Prentiss Brown be remembered?
A. He was the "Father of the Mackinac Bridge"
B. He was nominated to be Franklen Roosevelt's Vice President in 1940
C. He was the first U.S. Congressman from the Upper Peninsula

THE ANSWER IS A, B AND C AND MUCH MORE

Born in 1889 in St. Ignace, Michigan, Brown was first a prosecuting Attorney then elected U.S. Congressman in 1932, the first from the U.P. After the stock market crash he was instrumental in establishing the F.D.I.C., he drafted the law creating the Civilian Conservation Corp and supported many of FDR's New Deal programs.

He was appointed to the United States Senate in 1936 by Governor Frank Fitzgerald (On the recommendation of State Senator James Milliken, Gov. William Milliken's father) to fill the term after the death of Sen. James Couzens. He disagreed with Roosevelt on his court packing scheme, and fought him on it. Still, in 1940 he was nominated to be FDR's running mate, but turned it down.

He pushed for many years to build the Mackinac Bridge, finally. He was chair of the Mackinac Bridge Authority for many years.

Sen. Prentiss Brown, the man who all Michigan should remember, died at his home in St. Ignace in 1973 at age 84.

Why

In Southeastern Lower Michigan's Pokagon Township a former church, the First Methodist Episcopal Church of Pokagon, has been restored. It is now called, "The Old Rugged Cross Church." It is named for the hymn written by Reverend George Bennard, and first performed by a choir of five, accompanied by a guitar in that church in 1913.

Why did "The Old rugged Cross Church" need to be restored?

A. It had been abandoned in 1924
B. A local farmer bought it to be a cattle barn
C. It had turned into a general store

THE ANSWER IS B

In 1915 the church was sold to a local farmer who turned the church into a cattle barn. He took out the sanctuary's floor boards, and the building was used to house farm animals for more than 80 years. By 1998, the Old Rugged Cross Foundation decided to do something about it and began the restoration. Don't feel bad or like that old church was disrespected because it was used to house animals; if the farmer had not turned the old church into a barn it likely would not have survived.

In 2011 the mostly restored church was rededicated with the installation of the church's original bell and rope wheel. Rev. George Bennard was born in 1873, and died at his retirement home in Reed City, Michigan in 1958 at age 85. Reed City has a museum dedicated to his life and ministry.

In 1837 a group of investors, including Henry Schoolcraft and Michigan's first Governor Stevens T. Mason, bought some land in what is now Bay City. It was called Lower Saginaw. By 1843 a new group of investors came in, one of the investors, James G. Birney, was a nationally well-known attorney.

Why was James G. Birney well known?

A. He ran for President in 1840 and 1844
B. He was a famous abolitionist
C. He invented the lead pencil

THE ANSWER IS A & B

James Birney was Bay City's only Presidential nominee. An attorney and abolitionist from Kentucky; he had been a member of the Kentucky Legislature from 1816-1818 and, when he moved to Alabama in 1818 became a member of the Alabama Legislature; by 1829 he was Mayor of Huntsville, Alabama. He moved to Cincinnati, Ohio in 1836 and founded an abolitionist newspaper called The Philanthropist.

He was nominated by the Liberty Party for President in 1840 and 1844. He didn't get a lot of votes, but likely took enough votes from Henry Clay that he may have thrown the election to James Polk. He even received votes in the 1845 election for Governor of Michigan.

In 1841 James Birney came to Michigan and became a partner in the new Saginaw Bay Company becoming very involved in the planning of Bay City. Bay City's Birney Park is named for him. He lived in Bay City until 1855 when his health forced him to move east.

His son, James Birney, came to Bay City then called Lower Saginaw to take care of his father's business interests in the city. James remained in Bay City and is buried in Pine Ridge Cemetery.

Why

Bay City's original name was Lower Saginaw.
Why was it called Lower Saginaw?

A. Because it is below Saginaw on the Map
B. Because the Legislature didn't like Bay City
C. Because larger ships couldn't get to Saginaw

THE ANSWER IS C

Bay City was originally known as "Lower Saginaw." Saginaw was the first to be settled in 1819, but larger ships couldn't navigate the shallower water near the Saginaw settlement, so, the ships had to dock down river, or, the lower river.

In 1857, the name was changed to Bay City. Two years later, they incorporated Bay City as a village. Bay City became a city in 1865. In 1846 the first post office to serve "Lower Saginaw" was actually the Hampton post office.

At Lake Erie Metropark, in Brownstown just south of Detroit, on land that was once a Wyandotte Native American Village, stands a monument with two eight ton guns, and eight marble plaques. They are a memorial to a battle the Battle of Brownstown that Americans lost in the War of 1812.

The monument was constructed in 1908, to commemorate the battle and surrender of Fort Detroit by General William Hull. That Gen. Hull was court martialed and sentenced to death after he surrendered the fort, on August 12 1812, without a shot being fired was beside the point. President James Madison commuted the sentence because of his exemplary service during the Revolution.

A Detroit doctor decided, on his own, that General Hull deserved better. So he built the monument. Besides it being a little odd to commemorate a major defeat, there is something that is not right about the monster guns.

Why are the guns chosen to commemorate a battle of the war of 1812 a little odd?

    A.   The guns are too big
    B.   The guns are fake
    C.   The guns were cast 70-80 years after the War of 1812

THE ANSWER IS C

While they are big guns, they are real. The two Rodman guns, weighing eight tons each, were cast well after the War of 1812; in fact they were cast after the Civil War. When Dr. Hal Wyman, of Detroit, petitioned the federal government for an 1812 gun for the monument, they had nothing, so, they sent him the two Rodmans, which he accepted.

The plaques are also problematic as they are not very accurate, with miss-information and miss-spellings. The plaques were remade as originally written when the monument was restored and moved in 2004.

Roberta Applegate was born in Idaho and came to Michigan to attend Michigan State College, (now Michigan State University). Her name should be remembered, especially by women. She was a pioneer and leader.

Why should Roberta Applegate be remembered?

A. She was the first woman press secretary for a Michigan Governor
B. She was the first woman to operate an automobile dealership
C. She was the first woman to become a Michigan State Police Trooper

THE ANSWER IS A

Roberta "Bobbie" Applegate went to MSU to earn a Journalism Degree. Her father was a professor at MSU and a former newspaper editor. She reported on sports, clubs, politics, and hard news. She worked for the Associated Press during WWII when many men were overseas. She was the first woman to report on the governor and state politics in Michigan. She became the Press Secretary, the first woman to hold that position, to Governor Kim Sigler in 1948. Bobbie Applegate said that she knew she was being accepted by the other members of the press when they stopped apologizing to her when they cussed.

She ended up, like her father, a college professor at Kansas State University. Roberta Applegate died in 1990 at age 79.

The Village of Newberry, in Michigan's Upper Peninsula is a gateway to Tahquamenon Falls, the largest waterfall in the state. It is surrounded by state and national forests and is a great place to hunt and enjoy the outdoors. Newberry was founded in 1890 and was designated Michigan's "Moose Capital" by the Michigan Legislature in 2002.

Why was it named Newberry

A. For all the berries that the moose eat
B. For Detroit attorney John Newberry
C. It's a corruption of the French word Neu-beurrie, meaning lost place

THE ANSWER IS B

Newberry; Michigan is named for John Newberry from New York, a graduate of the University of Michigan Law School, a one term U.S. Congressman (1879-1881) a Detroit Attorney, a publisher of the Detroit Post and a supporter of Detroit's Harper Hospital. He was also an investor in the railroads that would haul lumber from Newberry to the Soo Locks.

Newberry was named for him, and many of the streets named for his children. When he died in 1887 he likely had never seen the town that bears his name.

Bay City has been a center of human activity for centuries. The first person of European decent, in Bay City, was probably Leon Trombley, who arrived in 1832 from Detroit.

Why did Leon Trombley come to Bay City?

    A.   He was going to teach Indians to farm
    B.   He came for lumber
    C.   He had escaped from the Wayne County Jail
    D.   He won a land lottery

THE ANSWER IS A

Leon Trombley was sent by the government from Detroit, Michigan in 1832, to teach the Indians agricultural methods. The problem was Trombley was not a farmer. As a matter of fact, many of the "agents" the Government sent to teach farming weren't farmers. Plus the Chippewa had been growing squash and maize for centuries.

Since he couldn't teach farming, and the Indians really didn't need the teachers, he decided to stay in the area and built a trading post on the banks of the Saginaw. A replica of that trading cabin is at Veterans Memorial Park in Bay City.

The Kirtland's warbler, also called the Jack Pine Warbler, is a rare and endangered species in Michigan. It was nearly extinct by the mid 1960's but has been making a steady comeback. It is a fascinating songbird that nests only in a very few areas in northern Michigan, and winters in the Bahama's; what a life.

Why has the Kirtland's Warbler been able to make a comeback since 1965?

    A.   More forest fires
    B.   Lumber companies no longer cut the trees
    C.   DDT is no longer used in the Great Lakes

Why

THE ANSWER IS A

The Kirtland Warbler is a songbird that nests exclusively under, and in the lowest branches of young Jack Pine Trees. Once the trees get to a certain height they no longer give protection to the nests. What they need is a good fire! Jack Pine cannot grow without a fire to start the process.

Firefighting and suppression practically stopped all fires, so the Kirtland's Warbler began to disappear. Today fires are set and controlled to keep the population of the Kirtland's Warbler on the upswing. Fire removes older trees and rejuvenates the forest, plus the heat opens jack pine cones so it can release its seeds. Fire also prepares the ground for the germination of the seeds.

Grayling Lumber Baron Rasmus Hanson founded the Grayling Fish Hatchery, in 1914. In 1926 it was sold to the State of Michigan who ran it as a fish hatchery and tourist attraction until the 1960's when it was closed. In 1995 Crawford County acquired the hatchery and it still is a fish farm and tourist attraction.

Why did Rasmus Hanson decide to found a fish hatchery in Grayling?

A.   He liked to fish
B.   He wanted to restock the Grayling
C.   He felt guilty about killing all the fish

THE ANSWER IS B

He wanted to restore the famous Grayling to the Au Sable River. The truth was it was logging that had caused the disappearance of the Grayling in the mid to late 1800's. Mr. Hanson, (1846–1927), had support from some pretty well known people in building the hatchery; including Henry Ford, Edsel Ford, and Thomas Edison.

Sadly, it didn't work. The Grayling never returned to the Au Sable, but the hatchery continues to hatch fish.

Olympia Brown was born in Schoolcraft, Michigan in 1834. She was so well known in her day that she had a school named for her, as well as a church and was named a member of the Michigan Women's Hall of Fame.

Why was Olympia Brown so well known?

Why

A. She was the first woman to be an ordained minister
B. She was first female captain of a Great Lakes schooner
C. She was the first woman who was elected Mayor of a Michigan City

THE ANSWER IS A

The Reverend Olympia Brown was the first woman to be ordained by a denominational church in the United States; the Unitarian Church. She was also a suffragette and knew and worked with Susan B. Anthony, Elizabeth Cady Stanton and others to get women the right to vote. She was one of the few early suffragists who lived to vote. She voted for the first time, with all women, in 1920 at the age of 85.

Why

"How?"

THE *(even)* GREATER, GREAT LAKES *(How)* TRIVIA QUIZ

The Atherton School District in the City of Burton was founded in 1836 as a one room school, before Michigan was even a state. By 1878 there were 8 elementary schools and 17 teachers in the Atherton District. In 2013 there were 3 buildings with around 900 students.

How did the Atherton School district get its name?

A. Named for Adonijah Atherton, one of the first area settlers.
B. It was named for Betsey Atherton the first teacher in the first school in 1836.
C. Named for the Ather River that used to run through the area.

ANSWER IS A AND B

The Atherton School District in Genesee County's City of Burton was named for the first school teacher in the district, Miss Betsey Atherton whose father Adonijah was one of the first settlers.

Spoon River Anthology is one of the most important poems in American literature. It later was adapted to become one of the most performed stage plays. On its publication in 1915 Edgar Lee Masters established himself as a leading American Poet.

The story is about the dead in a cemetery in a fictional town who tell their stories, warts and all. Many of the characters are easy to identify as neighbors of Masters in the town where he grew up, and many of them didn't like it.

How is Spoon River Anthology connected with Michigan?

A. Spoon River Anthology is really the story of Kalamazoo
B. Masters was born in Michigan
C. Spoon River Anthology was written in Michigan

THE ANSWER IS C

Spoon River Anthology was written in 1914 while Masters was staying in a house on Spring Lake, Michigan near the dunes of Lake Michigan.

Masters was an attorney who worked in the famous Clarence Darrow's office in Chicago. While the Town of Spoon River is fictional, the Spoon River is an actual river that runs near Master's childhood home town near Lewistown and Petersburg, Illinois.

How

How

Today you go into a grocery store, whether it's a national chain like Kroger and Walmart, or a more regional store like Meijer, you will find a pharmacy as well as your milk and eggs. But it wasn't always that way.

How did pharmacies become part of grocery stores in Michigan?

A. A grocery store owner in Detroit had a cousin who was a pharmacist
B. A drug store owner in Battle Creek wanted to sell some milk in his pharmacy
C. Michigan's Governor wanted to get groceries and prescription at the same time.

THE ANSWER IS A

The first grocery store in Michigan to also host a pharmacy was a small market in Detroit owned by Chaldeans, a people who came from northern Iraq. Thomas Hakim owned a store near Grand Boulevard in Detroit in the late 1950's. When he visited an Arizona grocery store he noted they had a pharmacy. He had a cousin who was a pharmacist and thought it would be a profit maker in his store, but it was illegal to have a pharmacy in a grocery store in Michigan.

He negotiated with the state and the Hakim Food and Drug Center was born. Today all the big chains use Mr. Hakim's idea, and us consumers appreciate the convenience.

We know that the first European ship to be lost on the Great Lakes was the Griffon, built by French explorer René-Robert Cavelier, Sieur de La Salle. That ship sank, on it's first voyage in Lake Michigan, on the Wisconsin side in 1679.

There's no way to get an exact number, but since that shipwreck there have been many, many more, from the Daniel J. Morrell to the Edmund Fitzgerald.

How many ships are guesstimated to have gone down on the Great Lakes?

A. 3,800
B. 6,000
C. 13,000

THE ANSWER IS B
While it is impossible to know exactly how many ships have sunk on the Great Lakes, the Great Lakes Shipwreck Museum estimates the number at 6,000 lost vessels and 30,000 lost lives.

Governor Stevens T. Mason was Michigan's first governor, serving from 1835-1840. He died at age 32 in 1843 in New York City, of pneumonia. The story about what happened to his body after he died is long and fascinating. He was moved and reburied several times before finally finding his final resting place.

How many times has the body of Gov. Stevens T. Mason been buried?

A. Two
B. Four
C. Seven

THE ANSWER IS B
Michigan's first Governor, Stevens T. Mason was buried 4 times;

- First, in 1843 in the City of New York where he died,
- Then in 1905 his remains were sent to Detroit where they were interred in Capital Park, the site of Michigan's first capital,
- In 1955 the body was moved to make way for a bus station on the site. They didn't know that he had been moved again until 2009 when officials decided to remake the park and to move Governor Mason's body, again. But he wasn't there! It took four days to find the body.
- On October 27, 2010, the 199th anniversary of his birth, the Governor was reburied for the fourth time in a newly built grave in another part of Capital Park.

Before his final, or latest, burial Governor Mason's remains were taken to Lansing where they lay in state in the Capitol Building. Mason was only the third Michigan governor to lie in state in the Capitol.

How

How did Benzonia and Benzie, as in Benzie County, get its name?

    A. It was just made up by Henry Schoolcraft.

    B. The English settlers couldn't pronounce the real name.

    C. It was named for Ben Zoney, the inventor of the Zamboni machine.

THE ANSWER IS B

The name "Benzie" came from the French Riviere Aux-Bec Scies or "river of sawbill ducks" (bec-scie)…and the English always have trouble pronouncing French words, so it sounded like Benzie, or Betsy. It was named for the ducks.

    They called it the Betsie River, which is where we got Benzie…or Benzonia.

Frankfort is the largest community in Benzie County. It was founded 1852 when Joseph Oliver built a small cabin on 14 acres he bought. It is well known for its harbor, at the outlet of the Benzie River on Lake Michigan.

    How was the Harbor of Frankfort discovered?

    A. Captain Snow accidentally found it when his ship wrecked in a storm

    B. Native Americans used it as a meeting place.

    C. French Missionaries found it while converting the Natives to Christianity

THE ANSWER IS A

In 1855 a schooner owned by George W. Tifft of Cleveland was caught in a gale on Lake Michigan and driven by the wind into the shore. Captain Snow was surprised when he found a previously little known river outlet and harbor which provided a safe refuge.

    Later Mr. Tifft purchased most of the land in the area and began to improve the harbor.

The Indianapolis 500 is one of the most famous automobile races in the world. The track itself was born in 1909 when a gravel-and-tar track was built and hosted small events, including motorcycles races.

    How is Michigan connected with the first Indy 500 in 1911?

A. It was won by a Michigan Driver
B. It was won by a car made in Michigan
C. It was sponsored by Buick

THE ANSWER IS A

The winner of the first Indianapolis 500 was Ray Harroun of Saginaw. Harroun was an engineer who worked for many years, after his win, at Saginaw Products Company. He won in a car called the "Marmon Wasp" because of its yellow color. The average speed was 75 miles per hour, which was really moving in 1911. Harroun never raced again.

There is also a connection to Buick as well. For the two years before the first Indianapolis 500, they ran the Prest-O-Lite Trophy Race at the Indianapolis Motor Speedway. That event was won in 1909 by another Michigan driver, driving a Buick. Wild Bob Burman was born in Imlay City, Michigan and spent part of his early life working in Kingston. For more on auto racing pioneer Bob Burman check out my book, "Michigan's Thumb Drive."

The Great Lakes are the defining feature of the Great Lakes State. They surround Michigan with freshwater and influence the weather, industry, and culture of the Great Lakes State.

How deep is the average depth of the shallowest of the Great Lakes?

A. 62 feet
B. 210 feet
C. 850 feet

THE ANSWER IS A

Lake Erie is the smallest and shallowest of the Great Lakes. Its average depth is 62 feet. At Erie's deepest point it is only 210 feet deep. Erie is the first lake to freeze in winter and the first to thaw in spring.

The Moravian Church is one of the oldest Protestant denominations in the world, dating back to 1457 in Europe. It was first established in America in 1735. They are called Moravians because the first members in Eastern, Germany in the 1720s came from Moravia. Moravians are also known as the Unity of Brethren. There are a million Moravians around the world.

The first Moravians in Michigan arrived in 1782 to man a Chippewa Indian Mission near Mt. Clemens. That was the first Protestant Church in Michigan, but it didn't last. The Moravian Church in Unionville is the oldest in Michigan, founded in 1870.

How did the Moravian Church come to be in Unionville?

A. A lumberjack found a piece of paper he happened to read.
B. The leader of the Church married the local grocer's daughter
C. A local businessman gave land to the Moravians so they would come to the area.

THE ANSWER IS A

The story goes that Philip Schichling, a lumberjack, picked up a piece of paper in his travels. He read the slip of paper and found that it came from a Moravia publication. He wondered who in this remote place would have left this piece of paper behind. He found it was left by a young school teacher whose father was a church member back in her native New York. That was the beginning. Today there are only three Moravian Congregations in Michigan.

The largest of the Great Lakes is Superior. With 2,800 miles of shoreline and 3,000 cubic miles of water, Superior is a big lake.

How deep is Superior's deepest point?

A. 750 feet deep
B. 925 feet deep
C. 1,332 feet deep

THE ANSWER IS C

At Lake Superior's deepest point it reaches a depth of 1,332 feet. Superior's average depth is 500 feet. It is a deep and cold lake. By the way the next deepest lake is Lake Michigan; its deepest point is 925 feet, the average depth 279 feet. Lake Huron's average depth is 195 and deepest point is 750 feet. Lake Erie is the shallowest with an average depth 62 feet and its deepest point 210 feet.

Muskrats are not rats at all, they are aquatic rodents related to voles and lemmings. They are native to North America and have been introduced to Europe and Asia and even South America. The name probably came from a Native American word for red, and for the musky smell it marks its territory with. They live much of their life in the water and can swim under water for 12 to 17 minutes.

In Monroe, Michigan muskrats are famous. In the 1890's Monroe was known, by some, as "Muskrat Town", or "Muskrat City."

How did Monroe get the nickname "Muskrat Town"?

A. Muskrats inundated Monroe in 1885 during a flood
B. A businessman sold fur coats made from Muskrat
C. People in the area were starving and ate Muskrat to save their lives

THE ANSWER IS C
During the war of 1812 both British and American troops were in the area. They fought at the Battle of the River Raisin. There were so many soldiers that they ate all the crops of local farmers and cut down the fruit trees for fuel. It was a starving time for the people of Monroe, it was especially hard on the many French Catholics in the area. Catholics had to abstain from eating meat on Fridays. They do have a lot of Muskrats, and muskrats live in the water, so, doesn't that make them fish? Not exactly, but the Catholic Church did give dispensation to eat muskrat on Fridays. So that is what they ate, muskrat later became a delicacy and treat for the citizens of the area.

Auto pioneer C.S. Mott's Applewood Estate, near downtown Flint, was called by Mr. Mott a "gentleman's farm." It was built 1916 on 65 acres. It had gardens, a brick barn, draft horses, cows, pigeons, chickens, ducks, pheasant and pigs. The estate is also known for its namesake apple orchard that contains many heritage varieties of apples.

Mott's family in New York, were farmers, he called them sodbusters, who operated a family cider and vinegar business. The Mott name is still used on a popular applesauce. Mr. Mott's family in New York sold the business and name years ago.

How many varieties of apples can you find in the orchard at C.S. Motts' Applewood Estate?

A. 50
B. 29
C. 17

THE ANSWER IS A

There are about 50 varieties of apples at Applewood. There are 29 heritage apple trees on site, some that are not available anywhere else.

Much of the original farm was given to the people of Flint and today it is the site of the Mott Community College Campus. Mr. Mott's home is now a museum operated by the Ruth Mott Foundation.

The Great Lakes make up 85% of the fresh water in the United States, and 1/5th of the world's fresh water. That is a lot of water and a great responsibility to maintain.

If the water in the Great Lakes flooded the 48 contiguous states how deep would the water be?

A. 14 inches
B. 9.5 feet
C. 16.2 feet

THE ANSWER IS B

If you were able to take all of the water from all of the Great Lakes and flooded the U.S. there would be about 9.5 feet of water from ocean to ocean.

The popularity of bow fishing is increasing on Michigan waters. It is big fish that are taken in bow fishing, like suckers. One variety of sucker is black buffalo. In September of 2012 a state record black buffalo was taken in backwaters of the Kalamazoo River with a bow.

How big was that state record black buffalo fish?

A. 33pound 4oz   36.5 inches
B. 37pound 4oz 39.4 inches
C. 41pound 2oz   42 inches

THE ANSWER IS B

We do have some big fish in Michigan waters. Bryan DeGoede shot the record 37.4 pound fish. His record black buffalo was much larger than the previous record 33.4 pounder caught in 2004. Black buffalo are found in the state's big rivers, the Kalamazoo, Grand and St. Joseph. They are also found in larger lakes such as Muskegon Lake, and Lakes Erie and St. Clair. As the popularity of bow fishing grows experts at the Michigan DNR expect that record to be broken as well.

Old Tiger stadium had several names through the years. In 1961 when owner John Fetzer bought the team and stadium he changed the name to Tiger Stadium from Briggs Stadium. Walter Briggs had named it for himself when he bought the team from Frank Navin, who had also named the stadium after himself. When Mr. Navin bought the team and stadium he changed the name from Bennett Field.

How did old Tiger Stadium get the name Bennett Field in 1911?

A. Named for another owner
B. Named for Governor Bennett a famous Michigan politician.
C. Named for a great player

How

THE ANSWER IS C

Believe it or not the owner, George Arthur Vanderbeck, named the stadium for a great player, something that is just unheard of. Charlie Bennett born in 1854 was a catcher who played eight seasons with the Detroit Wolverines from 1881-1888. He played during every season that the franchise existed and was the most popular ballplayer in 19th Century Detroit. He is also said to be the first player ever to take a curtain call.

Bennett lost both legs in a terrible train accident in 1893 and never played again. After his injury, Bennett moved to Detroit, where he operated a cigar store.

When a new ballpark opened in Detroit in 1896, it was named Bennett Park in his honor. Bennett caught the first pitch at Bennett Park in 1896. It was a tradition for Bennett to catch the first pitch in Detroit every season, an honor that Bennett continued until he died in Detroit in 1927 at age 72.

Beaver pelts were one of Michigan's first exports. Native American and the French trappers traveled great distances into the wilderness to get them. They were used to make hats for rich Europeans.

How did beaver hats become popular?

A. Cardinal Richelieu needed to tax them for income
B. Ben Franklin wore them
C. Louis XIII wore a beaver hat to keep warm at Versailles

THE ANSWER IS B

Beaver hats became famous in Europe when they were worn by Ben Franklin. Franklin was as famous then as any star is today, a scientist, philosopher, printer, and politician. Dr. Franklin was followed and quoted by what today would be called paparazzi. What he wore and what he said became famous as did the popularity of beaver hats.

The Great Fires of 1871 and 1881 in Michigan caused untold death and destruction. Both started in a drought stricken summer and were encouraged by piles of dry lumber scraps left by loggers.

How long did the Great Fire of 1871 last?

A. 8 days
B. 8 weeks
C. 8 months

THE ANSWER, STUNNINGLY, IS C

In 1903 Roswell Surine, an early settler in Unionville wrote a story in his home town newspaper, "The Unionville Crescent" about what life was like when he came to town in 1862. In that story he writes, "During the fire of 1871 I spent three weeks that I worked three days. The rest of the time I was fighting the fire." The fire of 1871 burned from June till January.

Tiger Great Al Kaline reached a baseball milestone in 1974, his 3,000 hit. For a player, 3,000 hits is usually a ticket to the Hall of Fame.

How long had it been since a baseball player reached 3,000 hits when Al Kaline collected number 3,000 in 1974?

A. 3 years
B. 22 years
C. 49 years

THE ANSWER IS C
When Hall of Famer Al Kaline collected hit number 3,000 in 1974 it had been 49 years since the last player had reached that plateau. That was Eddie Collins, a second baseman, manager and executive. He played from 1906 to 1930 for the Philadelphia Athletics and Chicago White Sox. He hit his 3,000th hit in 1925 for the White Sox and became a Hall of Famer in 1939.

John Southgate was born in England in 1856. In 1875 he came to America and Bay Port, Michigan in the Thumb, to become a commercial fisherman. He and his son both worked the waters of Lake Huron, and Saginaw Bay off of the Thumb for decades.

How big was the biggest fish he and his son ever caught?

A. 71 pounds
B. 141 pounds
C. 203 pounds

THE ANSWER IS B
In 1910 John Southgate caught a six and a half foot, 141 pound Lake Sturgeon in Saginaw Bay. There is even a photo of the giant fish. You can find it in 125 Years of Family Life & Progress in Unionville. The photo was first published in the Unionville Crescent May 13, 1910. The sturgeon is the largest ever reported caught in Saginaw Bay.

1951 was the beginning of the first ice taxi service on Saginaw Bay, and maybe anywhere. Art Beatenhead, a farmer, bought a Model A Ford Coupe, stripped it down and fitted it out for ice. The taxi would take fishermen out on the ice and would haul your, or a rented, fish shanty out as well. Beatenhead also had a pretty good business pulling the cars of those who didn't use his service; out of the water after they went through the ice.

How many vehicles, on average, did he pull out of the water between 1952 and 1961?

How

A.   4 a year
B.   13 a year
C.   26 a year

THE ANSWER IS C
During the decade he was in business Beatenhead pulled a minimum of 26 cars a year out of the water after they went through the ice of Saginaw Bay.

The story is famous in the auto industry and around Michigan. Billy Durant and J. Dallas Dort decide to go into the auto business and parley their carriage business into what would become General Motors. It all started with a loan.

How much did Billy Durant and J. Dallas Dort borrow to begin their Flint Road Cart Company?

A. $2,000
B. $12,000
C. $20,000

THE ANSWER IS A
Robert Whaley, President of Citizens Bank in Flint for 40 years made a loan for $2,000 to Durant and Dort in 1886. That $2,000 was the beginning of General Motors.
   Citizens Bank would operate for another 126 years in Flint until it was taken over by an Ohio Bank.

U.S. Presidents are often seen on college campuses to speak at commencements. At some of the country's great universities many presidents have addressed graduates, and other groups.

How many Presidents have spoken on the Ann Arbor campus of the University of Michigan?

A.   4
B.   8
C.   13

THE ANSWER IS C

As of 2013, 13 U.S. Presidents have spoken at the University of Michigan. Those would include; President Obama in 2010, the fourth U.S. President to give the commencement speech. Among others; President Lyndon Johnson talked about his 'Great Society' in 1964. President Gerald Ford spent a lot of time on campus as a student, but he also spoke as President as did President Bill Clinton. Grover Cleveland was between terms when he spoke at UM in 1892. John Kennedy introduced his "Peace Corp" plan in 1960 and Teddy Roosevelt called his 1899 visit a, "Corking good time."

How did Minnesota which became a state in 1858, 20 years after Michigan, get frontage on Lake Superior?

A. Bought it from Canada
B. Stole it from Wisconsin
C. In a treaty with the Winnebago Indian Tribe

THE ANSWER IS B

While Wisconsin was in process of becoming a state in 1848, Congress was already thinking about the future State of Minnesota. So, Congress set aside Lake Superior frontage for Minnesota to; "Provide a more equitable division of resources."

Buick was founded by David Buick in 1903. Later that year the Flint Wagon Works, Billy Durant and J.Dallas Dort, purchased Buick and moved it to Flint. In 1904 the New Buick Motors began production. How many Buicks were produced that first year in Flint?

A. 37
B. 723
C. 12,685

THE ANSWER IS A

Billy Durant took charge of Buick in November 1904 and 37 vehicles were built that year. Almost 16 million Buicks were built in Flint between 1907 and 1999.

How

They call them sugar maples. They are the trees that are tapped in the spring to get the sap that is boiled down into maple syrup. Making maple syrup is something that has been done in Michigan since the first people arrived.

How many sugar maple trees are estimated to be in Michigan?

    A.   One million
    B.   150 million
    C.   275 million

THE ANSWER IS C

It is estimated that there are 275 million sugar maple trees in Michigan. That would make a lot of syrup, but only about 1% are tapped for syrup. According to Michigan growers, while Michigan has more sugar maple trees than Quebec, Canada, but Quebec makes 80-85% of all the maple syrup in the world.

How much did the grandson of auto pioneer Henry Ford, William Clay Ford, pay for the Detroit Lions Football team?

    A. $7,952
    B. $4.5 million
    C.   28 million

THE ANSWER IS B

William Clay Ford bought the Lions for $4.5 million in 1963.

In 1934 a group of investors first brought the Lions to Michigan from Portsmouth. Ohio. They paid $7,952 for the team. Today it is estimated to be worth closer to a billion dollars.

The University of Michigan is one of the oldest and most prestigious schools in the US. For more than a century U of M has been known as a football school, but, it has been a baseball school for almost as long.

How many University of Michigan Wolverines are members of the Baseball Hall of Fame?

A. 5
B. 7
C. 12

THE ANSWER IS A

Four "Michigan Men" earned a spot in the Baseball Hall of Fame in Cooperstown, New York. The latest was Barry Larkin from Kalamazoo, Michigan, who was inducted in 2012. He came to play football but decided his future was in baseball, so he left the football team. Football Coach Bo Schembechler didn't like it much. Larkin quoted him as saying, "No one comes to Michigan to play stinking baseball." Guess he was wrong about that.

The other wolverines in the Baseball Hall of Fame;

Branch Rickey who was inducted in 1967. He loved the game, and played for many years, but was better known as a baseball executive. He attended the Michigan Law School and coached the Michigan Baseball team. As a baseball executive he was the man who signed Jackie Robinson to a major league contract, breaking the color barrier and changing the game forever.

Charlie Gehringer was inducted into the Hall of Fame in 1949. He was known to Detroit Tiger fans as the "Mechanical Man" because he was practically perfect in the field. He played for the Wolverines for one year, signed with the Tigers and played 18 years. His lifetime average is 320; he played for 3 league champions and one World Series Champion in 1935.

George Sisler, the only graduate of the University of Michigan who made the Hall of Fame was a left handed pitcher who was recruited to the Michigan baseball team by Coach Rickey. After graduation Rickey signed him for the St. Louis Browns as a first baseman. "Gorgeous George" was inducted in 1939 after a 15 year career that saw him hit 400 twice and set a league record with 254 hits that he held till Ichiro Suzuki topped it in 2004.

Larry MacPhail, from Cass City, Michigan went to the University of Michigan and attended George Washington University Law School where he met baseball innovator Branch Rickey. In 1933 he was hired by the Cincinnati Reds as general manager. He went on to serve as president/general manager of the Brooklyn Dodgers and the New York Yankees. Among MacPhail's innovations; nighttime baseball, regular game televising and the flying of teams between games. MacPhail was elected to the Baseball Hall of Fame in 1978. Larry MacPhail died in 1975 and is buried at Elkland Township in Cass City.

(Extra notes) His son **Lee MacPhail** was also a baseball man and President of the American League. He was elected to the Hall in 1998, making them the only father and son inductees to baseball's Hall of Fame. His grandson, Andy MacPhail, was born in 1953 and was general manager of the Minnesota Twins from 1986–1994, president/CEO of the Chicago Cubs from 1994–2006, and president/baseball operations of the Orioles from 2007–2011.

How

Larry's great grandson, Lee MacPhail III was an executive with the Reading Phillies of the Eastern baseball League when he died in an auto accident in 1969 at age 27. There is one more, Lee MacPhail IV, Andy's Son, has been a special assistant to the general manager for the Seattle Mariners

In downtown Flint the famous red bricks that cover a half mile of Saginaw Street, between Court Street and the Flint River, have been in place since the Great Depression, 1936.

They are the start and finish line for the world famous Crim Festival of Races 10 Mile Race, and are listed as part of a historic district, known as the "Saginaw Street Bricks."

How many bricks does it take; approximately, make up the Bricks of Saginaw Street?

    A.   Half a million
    B.   750,00
    C.   1.2 million

THE ANSWER IS B
Approximately 750,000 bricks were used to pave downtown Flint's Saginaw Street the half mile from Court Street to the Flint River.

Brick streets like Saginaw are unusual, and just a few remain in the state, according to the Michigan Department of Transportation, but they do exist. The positive; the bricks last many times longer than asphalt, and longer than concrete. The negative; they are expensive to fix.

The Detroit Lions uniform is the unique Honolulu Blue, and has been for years.

How did Honolulu Blue come to be the colors of the Detroit Lions?

    A.   George Richards, who owned WJR Radio, asked his wife for suggestions.
    B.   They found a special deal on shirts that had been dyed Honolulu Bblue
    C.   The owner let a player choose to get him to sign a contract.

THE ANSWER IS C

In 1934 George Richards brought the Portsmouth (Ohio) Spartans to Detroit. He had to pick a nickname and colors for his new team. All Pro running back Glenn Presnell was supposed to coach at West Virginia, but Richards made him an offer, he gave him a $4,000 salary and let him choose the team colors. Glenn Presnell and his wife chose the colors that the lions wear to this day.

Detroit was founded by French explorer Antoine de La Mothe de Cadillac in 1701. It was incorporated as a city almost one hundred years later, in 1802.

How many buildings were estimated to be in Detroit in 1802 when Detroit became a city?

A. 73
B. 300
C. 1,400

THE ANSWER IS B.

When Detroit was incorporated as a city in 1802 there were an estimated 300 buildings in the small town.

Michigan's lumber industry was big business forging wealth and communities. Moving the lumber was done in winter so the loads could run on frozen ground. Then, when they got to water the lumber went into the rivers to be floated to the mills.

Huge loads of lumber would be stacked on sleighs and hauled to the mill or river. At the Chicago World's Fair in 1893 they had a contest to see who could move the biggest load of lumber with two horses on a sleigh.

How heavy was the largest load of logs ever hauled by a two horse team on a sleigh?

A. 50 tons of lumber
B. 144 tons of lumber
C. 207 tons of lumber

How

THE ANSWER IS B

The Nester Estate in the Upper Peninsula had mills at Baraga on Lake Superior, and on the Sturgeon and Ontonagon Rivers. They were chosen by the Chairman of the Michigan Forestry Committee, Arthur Hill of Saginaw, to enter the contest.

The championship load, the most logs ever known to go on a single sleigh be pulled by two horses weighed 144 tons, was thirty feet high and 18 feet long and wide. There were 50 logs in ten layers, the largest at the bottom. The load totaled approximately 36,055 board feet.

Movie Director Francis Ford Coppola is known as the Academy Award winning director of such films as "The Godfather", Apocalypse Now", "The Cotton Club" and the Great Gatsby."

Born in Detroit, he was two when his family moved to New York.

How did Francis Ford Coppola's family end up in Detroit?

A. They came to work in the auto plants
B. His mother was a Detroit native
C. His father was a great musician

THE ANSWER IS C

His father, Carmine Coppola, was a flautist with the Detroit Symphony Orchestra. Francis' middle name, "Ford" was given in honor of Henry Ford. He was born at Henry Ford Hospital and his father was the arranger for the "Ford Sunday Evening Hour" on the radio.

They moved to New York when Carmine was named principal flautist for the NBC Orchestra.

In 1847, a decade after Michigan became a state the Legislature decided to move the capital out of the state's largest and most developed city, Detroit. There were several options debated including; Owosso, Jackson and Marshall, as well as the possibility of keeping the capital in Detroit. In the end they chose Lansing township, a place that had literally no roads or railroads.

How many times did they have to vote in the Michigan Senate before they finally made their decision?

A. 8
B. 27
C. 32

THE ANSWER IS B

After much contentious debate, on the record 27th vote the Michigan Senate accepted the House recommendation for the move. When the representatives arrived in the new capital seven months later they found a frame capital building, a hotel, the all-important tavern, a printing office, a few stores and houses and stumps still in the middle of the streets.

The small village of Glenn, on U.S 3I on Lake Michigan near South Haven, is also known as, "Pancake Town."

How did Glenn, Michigan become "Pancake Town?

A. Because of a huge snowstorm
B. Because Aunt Jemima was from there
C. Josephus Pan, a local cook, invented pancakes to serve to miners

THE ANSWER IS A

In December, 1937, one of the biggest snowstorms of the century hit. Massive snow drifts and blowing snow stranded people in 60 trucks and 100 cars. Glenn only had a diner, a gas station and an IGA. The people of Glenn took in the stranded motorists and fed them, but the IGA started to run out of food.

A new grocery store had been preparing to open and some of the food had begun to arrive before the storm hit, but the only supplies they had received was, you guessed it, boxes of pancake mix. Soon everybody was eating pancakes; national media was calling people in the town asking, "If the supply of pancakes was exhausted yet."

Three days of pancake eating later the roads were finally reopened, but the pancakes of Pancake Town weren't forgotten. They held a "Pancake Festival" for several years before WWII, and until 1963 after the war.

The actress who played Aunt Jemima (Clara Williams) made an appearance at the first festival in 1938. They still celebrate with a pancake dinner on occasion in "Pancake Town"; Glenn, Michigan.

How

When Detroit was founded along the Detroit River in 1701 land was sold and claimed in the French manner, in long strips or ribbons that started at the river and went a long way inland. One of the reasons this worked was it gave every land owner access to the river. Another positive is the 'ribbon farms" were close enough together they created a sense of community. There was at least one other important reason "ribbon farms" worked for the early settler on Detroit.

Besides access to water and social considerations, why did "ribbon farms" make sense for early settlers of Detroit?

A. Settlers could see all their land
B. They could come to each other's assistance quickly
C. It was much easier to mow a narrow lot

THE ANSWER IS B
Besides giving all settlers in Detroit access to the river for food and transportation, and for the social aspect of being able to have neighbors in the wilderness, the settlers were also able to come to each other's assistance or get to the fort in case of Indian attack

WWII started with Germany's invasion of Poland in 1939. It soon involved almost evry country on earth. Millions served and died in that war.

How many Michigan citizens served in the military during WWII?

A. 613,543
B. 937,626
C. 1.234 million

THE ANSWER IS A
613,543 Michiganians served during WWII. 29,321 were injured and 10,263 paid the ultimate sacrifice.

Boblo Island, on the Canadian side of the Detroit River was known as an amusement park for almost a century, till it closed in 1993.

How did Boblo Island get its name?

A. Named for Bob Lowenstein, the entrepreneur who built the amusement park
B. Corrupted from the French word, bois blanc, for trees native to the island
C. Named for a Native American game, bobapps, kind of like bobbing for apples.

THE ANSWER IS B

Boblo Island was named Bois Blanc by the first French explorers in the 1600's for the white trees on the island. Bois blanc is French for white wood, it may mean birch or basswood. Boblo was a stop on the famous Underground Railroad for slaves fleeing the south. As many as 30,000 former slaves were said to cross to Canada through Detroit.

Dick Tracy the square jawed law man famous in film, television and well as in comic books and newspaper strips was created by Chester Gould. Born in 1900, Gould would draw the strip for 46 (1931-1977) years from his home in Woodstock, Illinois.

How is Dick Tracy connected to Michigan?

A. Dick Tracy first appeared in a Detroit Newspaper
B. Chester Gould had a friend named Rick Tracy in Ontonagon
C. Dick Tracy's beat was Grand Rapids

THE ANSWER IS A

The first Dick Tracy comic strip appeared on October 4, 1931, in the Detroit Mirror. Dick Tracy's beat was actually in New York.

Women were not always welcome on college campuses. There were women's colleges, but, for the most part men went to their schools and women to theirs. The University of Michigan class of 1871 was the first to graduate both men and women.

How many women graduated in the University of Michigan Class of 1871?

How

A. I
B. 2
C. 22

THE ANSWER IS B

Only two women graduated in the first coed class at the University of Michigan.

The nation's first ever "commercial" aircraft show was held in Detroit in 1928. It was appropriate that the center of automobile industry in the U.S. would also be interested in aircraft; many of the auto companies were very involved in the aircraft industry. The show was held in the Detroit convention hall and was considered a "review of the American aeroplane industry."

How many planes were exhibited at the 1928 Detroit Aircraft Show?

A. 12
B. 37
C. 63

THE ANSWER IS C

63 aircraft were shown at the 1928 show which ran from April 11 through the 21st. According to Flight magazine, "no other nation can at present repeat the effort of over 40 firms appearing with more than 60 types for unsubsidized private flying." Among the planes on display, a 1909 Channel Bleriot monoplane, The Fokker " Super-Universal," with Pratt and Witney "Wasp " Engine and the Eastman Flying Boat.

During WWII the Japanese launched some 9000 balloon bombs they expected to float across the Pacific and start forest fires, cause explosions and wreck chaos and confusion in the Western US. They were the only way the Japanese could respond to the Doolittle raid on Tokyo.

How many of the WWII Japanese Balloon Bombs hit Michigan?

A. None

B. I

C. 5

THE ANSWER IS B

While the Japanese didn't expect they would get that far, a balloon bomb was found southeast of DeTour Village in the Upper Peninsula. It was reported in a Sault St. Marie newspaper in August 1945.

In the end the balloon bombs were a failure as a war measure. Two people were confirmed killed and a couple of brush fires started according to records.

In 1918, as men were being called up for the draft in WWI Dr. Simon Levin, in Houghton County, found that as many as 30 percent of the draftees were unfit, due to goiters, or growths in the neck. That was caused by their thyroid glands being swollen. As a matter of fact, goiters were common among many adults in Michigan as well. More draftees were disqualified for goiter than any other thing medical issue.

The problem was common in Michigan, but why so rare on the East Coast and West Coasts.

How did the goiter problem get solved in Michigan, and around the country?

A. Surgery to remove the goiters.

B. Add iodine to salt

C. A diet of vegetables

THE ANSWER IS B

Goiter is caused by a lack of iodine in our diet. On the Coasts they eat seafood, which has iodine and rain puts iodine in the soil, from the oceans. It was an idea that actually came from Switzerland. They solved their problem by adding potassium iodide to salt.

It was found that would be the least expensive and simplest way to get iodine into our diets, since most people eat salt every day. That is why our salt, "Pours when it rains" and has the words "iodized" on the label, and that is why goiters are practically non-existent today in Michigan, or anywhere in the country.

Ortonville is a small community in Oakland County, just south of the Genesee County Line.

How did Ortonville get its name?

A. For Amos Orton, Grist mill owner
B. Because of a boat factory in the area, whose motto was, "we make orrs by the ton."
C. For a French trapper known as O. R. Tonsett

THE ANSWER IS A

Ortonville was named for founder Amos Orton whose grist mill inspired people to settle and build in this area.

Tiger great Mickey Cochrane; a Tiger catcher and manager, at the same time! He led the Tigers to their first World Series win.

How are Detroit Tiger Hall of famer Mickey Cochran and the New York Yankees connected?

A. He was traded to the Yankees and helped them win their first World Series
B. One of the Yankees greatest stars was named for him
C. He was born in Detroit

THE ANSWER IS B

When Mickey Cochrane led the Philadelphia A's to Pennants over the Yankees from 1929 thru 1931, a man in Oklahoma was so impressed he named his son after him. His son's name was Mickey Mantle.

Born in Bridgewater, Massachusetts Mickey Cochrane is considered one of the best catchers of all time and is a member of the Baseball Hall of Fame. Made his debut in 1925, was A.L. MVP in 1928. He won 3 World Series, two with the A's, in 1929-30, and 1935 for the Tigers. Cochrane's career ended abruptly after a near-fatal head injury from a pitched ball in 1937. He served in the U.S. Navy in WWII. Cochrane died of cancer at age 59 in 1962.

After lumbermen clear cut timber from one end of Michigan to the other residents were left with piles of refuse and stumps, thousands and thousands of stumps. Those massive tree stumps left over from the white pine that were felled had stopped the development of farms.

In 1905 a company started to use dynamite to blast the stumps from the ground, which farmers liked because once the stumps were gone, they could plant crops. They had also found a way to make a profit on those huge stumps.

How did businessmen think they could make money from stumps?

A. They would make turpentine
B. Use them to build fences
C. They would fuel Great Lakes freighters

THE ANSWER IS A

In 1905 there was a market, especially in Europe, for Turpentine. Turpentine is made from the resin of live trees, especially pine trees. These entrepreneurs had figured out a way to get the resin by distilling old stumps that were blasted out of the ground.

By the 1910's there were several plants around the state, by 1915 the turpentine distilling boom was over, not because they ran out of stumps, you can still find some of those old huge stumps in the woods. They went out of business because WWI started and the European market dried up. A ten year boom went bust almost overnight.

Chuck Jones was a famous animator, cartoon artist, screenwriter, producer, and director of animated films. He was the brain behind the "Looney Tunes" and "Merrie Melodies" cartoons. Elmer Fudd, Pepe' Le Pew, Bugs Bunny, Daffy Duck, the Road Runner, Porky Pig and many more cartoon characters came from his head. He also drew Tom and Jerry shorts and created television's Dr. Seuss' "How the Grinch Stole Christmas."

How is Chuck Jones connected to Michigan?

A. He attended the University of Michigan
B. He created a character named Michigan J. Frog
C. The Character Elmer Fudd was based on a friend in Escanaba

THE ANSWER IS B

Of all the great cartoon characters, from Rikki Tikki Tavi, and Wile E. Coyote, to Bugs Bunny and Marvin the Martian, Chuck Jones favorite was one named "Michigan J. Frog"; a character created in his masterpiece, "One Froggy Evening", released in 1955. Steven Spielberg called "One Froggy Evening" Chuck Jones' "Citizen Caine."

"Michigan" was a song and dance frog who appeared in only two cartoons, and made a special appearance in, "Who Framed Roger Rabbit."

How did they come up with that name? Well, the only words in the entire six minute cartoon are songs sung by "Michigan" in an Al Jolson style. One of those songs was called; "The Michigan Rag." Chuck Jones was nominated for 10 Academy Awards, and won six. He died in 2002 at age 89.

WXYZ in Detroit famously produced many national radio shows, including; "The Lone Ranger" and "The Green Hornet" for broadcast throughout the US and Canada. These Michigan produced and written shows had an interesting connection.

How were the Lone Ranger and the Green Hornet connected?

A. The characters were blood relatives
B. They were written by the same man
C. They both wore masks

THE ANSWER IS A & C

As the story plays out, the Lone Ranger was the Green Hornet's Great Uncle. Of course they both wore masks. In the Lone Ranger saga John Reid (aka the Lone Ranger) is a Texas Ranger who survives an ambush that kills his brother, who was also a Texas Ranger. The Ranger raises his brother's son, and that son has a son named Brit. Brit is the Green Hornet.

Besides the masks and the fact they both were Detroit creations there are other similarities. The Lone Ranger had a sleek fast horse named "Silver, the Green Hornet had a sleek fast car named "Black Beauty", at a time of racial issues the Lone Ranger had an Indian sidekick named "Tonto", and the Green Hornet had a Japanese sidekick named "Kato."

Michigan Adventure's is a 250-acre amusement park on the west side of Michigan in Muskegon County. It is the largest amusement park in Michigan. It has over 50 rides, a water park and lots of activities.

How did Michigan Adventure's get started?

A. It was a u-pick berry farm
B. A small cemetery at a closed church
C. A deer park and petting zoo.

THE ANSWER IS C
Michigan Adventure opened in 1956 as a deer park and petting zoo with over 100 deer. The first ride was built in 1958, a 16 gauge train. Today it has seven roller coasters that will trill the enthusiast.

It's illegal to walk, ride a bike or a snowmobile across the Mackinac Bridge without special permission. They do make exceptions. Every year thousands walk across the mighty Mac on Labor Day, and occasionally a bike or snowmobile group is allowed to ride across.

How many snowmobiles crossed the Mackinac Bridge the first time they were allowed on the bridge?

A. 13
B. 117
C. 1,252

THE ANSWER IS A
The year is 1970 and for the first time the state gave a group of 13 snow machine riders permission to ride across the bridge.

Michigan was the arsenal of Democracy during WWII. Michigan manufacturers built planes, tanks, machine guns, airplane motors, army trucks and more. Not surprisingly with all the men overseas during the war the unemployment rate went way down.

How low did the unemployment rate in Michigan in WWII go?

A. 0%
B. 0.6%
C. 1.2%

How

THE ANSWER IS B

The Michigan unemployment rate dropped to 0.6% by 1944, a drop from 15% in 1940. That year only 12,000 people in Michigan were out of work. The national unemployment rate was 1.2%

The Kirtland Warbler is a Michigan songbird that nests in northern Michigan and winters in the Bahama's. It is on the endangered Species list, but has made a big comeback since it was almost extinct in the mid 1960's.

How did the Kirtland Warbler get its name?

A. It was named for Kirtland College in Roscommon
B. It was named for its discoverer, Jared P. Kirtland
C. It was named in memory of Ornithologist Prof. Kirt Land PhD.

THE ANSWER IS B

The Kirtland's Warbler was named for Dr. Jared Kirtland, a physician, teacher, naturalist and author who found one near Cleveland, Ohio in1851. That is when they still had forests around Ohio.

He wrote the book listing the birds, mammals, fishes, reptiles, and amphibians of Ohio. Dr. Kirtland sent that first specimen to the Smithsonian Institution in Washington, D.C.

If you wander into Michigan's Great North Country, and happen upon Grayling, you will likely see beautiful Lake Margrethe. Camp Grayling, the largest National Guard training facility in the country, is on the shore of the lake, as are many summer cottages.

How did Lake Margrethe get its name?

A. Named for Margrethe Hanson, wife of a local lumber baron
B. A dart was thrown at a list of names
C. It was drawn from a milk can in a lottery.

THE ANSWER IS A

Lake Margrethe was named for Margrethe Hanson, the wife of Lumber Baron Rasmus Hanson. Rasmus was born in Denmark in 1846 and came to this country at age 16. He made his fortune in lumber, and also owned the Michigan Sugar Company and the Bay City Sugar Company.

He donated the first chunk of land that became Camp Grayling National Guard base, has also built the Grayling Fish Hatchery. The lake was renamed in his wife's honor around 1913. Before it was Lake Margrethe, it was known as Portage Lake.

Houghton Lake is the largest natural inland lake in the state of Michigan, and one of the largest natural inland lakes in the United States. It is famous for fishing and boating in summer and for winter festivals like "Tip up Town" in winter. It has 31 miles of shoreline.

How far does Houghton Lake reach at its longest point from shore to shore?

    A.   4.5 miles
    B.   7.5 miles
    C.   11 miles

THE ANSWER IS B

At its longest point, north to south, Houghton Lake is 7.5 miles long. It is 4.5 miles across at its widest point east to west. Houghton Lake has 31 miles of shoreline and covers 20,044 acres

Michigan's first Governor, Governor Stevens T. Mason, was unique from every other Governor in Michigan history?

How was Gov. Mason different?

    A.   He was very short
    B.   He didn't know how to ride a horse
    C.   He was very young.

THE ANSWER IS C

He was very young. As a matter of fact, when he was named Secretary of the Michigan Territory by President Andrew Jackson in 1831, at age 19, he was too young to vote. He is considered the youngest presidential appointee in American history,

Stevens Thomson Mason was born on October 27, 1811. He was known as "The Boy governor" and called "Tom" by friends. In 1834 he was appointed acting Territorial Governor. He was elected governor of the state of Michigan at age 23 as a member of the Democratic Party in 1835, and served until 1840, the youngest state governor in American history.

In 1841, Mason left Michigan for New York City, to establish a law practice there. He died in the winter of 1843 at the age of thirty-one.

The Detroit Tigers have been playing baseball in Detroit since it was a founding member of the Western League in 1894. That league later became the American League.

How did the Tigers become, get their nickname, the Tigers?

A. Named by a newspaper
B. Named for a Detroit army regiment,
C. Named for the black and brown striped stockings they wore.

THE ANSWER IS A, WITH A LITTLE B

The Tigers were named by a Detroit Free Editor named Philip Reid on April 16, 1895. The headline he wrote that day; "Strouthers' Tigers Showed up Very Nicely." Strouthers was Con Strouthers the team manager. He just thought they had played like tigers.

In about 1900 the team asked the Detroit Light Guard Tigers, veterans of the Civil and Spanish American War, if they could also use the name Tigers.

In 1896 a new manager, George Stallings, claimed the nickname was his idea, after he made the team wear tiger striped socks. However the name had already been used for over a year with Stallings arrived in Detroit.

In some ways the Santa Claus we know today in popular culture was, at least partly, born in Michigan. The jolly old guy with a long white beard, rosy cheeks and twinkle in his eye a Michigan creation?

How is the Santa we recognize today, connected to Michigan?

A. William Kerr of Flint was the model for Santa
B. Haddon Sundblom of Muskegon drew him
C. Sam Tata of Calumet, Michigan gave him his name (He was St. Nicholas before)

THE ANSWER IS B

Haddon Hubbard "Sunny" Sundblom was an artist and illustrator who did advertising and magazine spreads. He was born in Muskegon in 1899; his parents came from Sweden.

He accepted a commission from the Coca Cola Company to come up with a Santa for their advertising campaign; for inspiration he read Clement Moore's 1822 poem, "A Visit From Saint Nicholas." Coke uses his image of Santa in its advertising to this day.

In the 1930's Sundblom began to do pin-ups and glamour calendars; his last assignment, in 1972, was a cover for Playboy Magazine!

William E. "Bill" Kerr Is the CEO of the Food Bank of Eastern Michigan; whose goal is to, "eradicate hunger within the community." The Food Bank is part of Feeding America, a national network of food banks and distributes food to those in need in 22 counties.

Bill is also a friend of the author from his hometown in Flint, and a fellow Eagle Scout. He is a Flint Southwestern and Michigan State University graduate. Bill is married to Jennifer and has three daughters and four grandchildren. Bill is an avid outdoorsman who says about his life; "I am one of the blessed people who love their job, what their job's mission is and who they work for and with.

As for Sam Tata; I have to admit, I just made that name up.

The great State of Michigan is home to many wonderful parks. Large and small, they are located from the tip of the Keweenaw to the Ohio border.

How did Maybury State Park, in Northville near Detroit, get its name?

A. Named for a tuberculosis asylum
B. Named for Andy Griffith's television home, Maybury RFD.
C. Named for Governor John Maybury

THE ANSWER IS A

Maybury State Park is named for William H. Maybury a real estate developer who developed land he owned in Northville into a tuberculosis asylum which was named for him in 1927. It kept his name when it became a state park in 1975.

Jacobsen Department Store was famous in Michigan for bringing New York items to the medium sized towns in Michigan, leaving the big city of Detroit to Hudson's. In 1939 the Jacobsen family sold the business, in Jackson, to Nathan Rosenfeld.

The Rosenfeld's put together a big advertising campaign to announce they were going to have a big sale to celebrate their new acquisition. It was going to be a huge sale on furs that would empty the fur vault at the store. But, there was a problem, right after the sale of the business, and the big fur sale the new owners realized that the only person who knew the vault combination was the nephew of the former owner, and he had gone on vacation. .

How did the new owners of Jacobsen Department Store get the vault open?

A. Sent the Sheriff out with a warrant for the nephew's arrest.
B. Hired a demolition crew to knock the vault down.
C. Borrowed a safecracker from a local prison.

THE ANSWER IS C

Mr. Rosenfeld called a friend he had met at a local Rotary Club meeting. It just so happened that this new friend was the Warden at Jackson Prison, the largest walled prison in the world. Rosenfeld asked him if he could borrow his best "safecracker."

The sale was a success after the convict opened the vault, The safecracker convict did earn himself a great breakfast in one of the fine restaurants in town before he was taken back to Jackson Prison.

How

"Friends
… they cherish one another's hopes.
They are kind to one another's dreams."
Henry David Thoreau

My deepest appreciation and thanks to my friends who have supported me in publishing this book, and so much more.

Michael Weber

Jeff & Pamela Payne

Chris Hamilton

Mike Lysher

Michael Kelly

Mark Businski

Lori Tallman Kendrick

William "Bill" Kerr

Stan Blood

Mark and Debbie Towar

Robert V. Jewell

Sharon Thorp

Charles Frederick Towar

Dave Crabill

Robert Schiller

Matt Schlinker

BIBLIOGRAPHY & ACKNOWLEDGEMENTS

Michigan Place Names: The History of the Founding and the Naming of More Than Five Thousand Past and Present Michigan Communities. Walter Romig, Wayne State University Press, 1973

Michigan History Magazine. The Historical Society of Michigan, Lansing, MI

Re-Thinking Michigan Indian History. LeBeau, Patrick Russell. Michigan State University. East Lansing, MI 2005

Indian Names in Michigan. Virgel Vogel. The University of Michigan Press, Ann Arbor, MI. 1986

Michigan Native Peoples. Marcia Schonberg. Heinemann Library, Chicago, Illinois. 2004

Geography of Michigan. John A. Dorr Jr. and Donald F. Eschman. University of Michigan Press. Ann Arbor, MI. 1970

A Drive Down Memory Lane: The Named Highways of Michigan. Leroy Barnett, PhD. The Priscilla Press Allegan Forest, Michigan 2004

Kingston, MI 1857-1982. Quasqui-Centennial, Kingston Historical Society, 1982 F.P. Horak Company, INC. Bay City, Michigan

Remembering Tuscola- A Pictorial History. Heritage House Publishing, Marceline, MO. 64658, Copyright 1992